An Answer to Disenfranchised Students:

High School Credit-Recovery and Acceleration Programs Increasing Graduation Rates for Disenfranchised, Disengaged, and At-risk Students at Nontraditional Alternative High Schools

Dr. Sharon D. Jones Deloach

Dissertation.com
Boca Raton, Florida
USA • 2016

An Answer to Disenfranchised Students: High School Credit-Recovery and Acceleration Programs Increasing Graduation Rates for Disenfranchised, Disengaged, and At-risk Students at Nontraditional Alternative High Schools

Dissertation.com
Boca Raton, Florida
USA • 2016

ISBN: 978-1-61233-446-2 (paperback)
978-161233-447-4 (ebook)

Library of Congress Control Number: 2016943283
Publisher's Cataloging-in-Publication Data

Names: Deloach, Sharon D. Jones
Title: An answer to disenfranchised students : high school credit-recovery and acceleration programs increasing graduation rates for disenfranchised, disengaged, and at-risk students at nontraditional alternative high schools / Sharon D. Jones Deloach.
Description: Boca Raton, FL : Dissertation.com, 2016.
Identifiers: ISBN 978-1-61233-446-2 (pbk.) | ISBN 978-1-61233-447-9 (ebook)
Subjects: LCSH: High school dropouts--United States--Prevention. | Problem youth--Education. | Alternative education. | Progressive education. | School credits. | School choice. | Academic achievement. | BISAC: EDUCATION / Non-Formal Education. | EDUCATION / Secondary.
Classification: LCC LC46.3 .D45 2016 (print) | LCC LC46.3 (ebook) | DDC 371.04--dc23.

CONTENTS

CHAPTER 5: RECOMMENDATIONS and IMPLICATIONS

REFERENCES

LIST OF FIGURES

PREFACE

It's nine-forty five in the evening and I find myself pondering about three students-Nat, Savana, and Colton. To protect the students' identity, I have changed their names. First there was Nat. Nat, was a struggling seventeen year old who had repeated ninth grade three times. In fact, he had a below fifth grade reading level, below fourth grade level in math, and had been identified as a learning disabled and behavioral student. As I sit here, I can visualize Nat with his bright smile, beautiful white teeth, and dimples that would surely win over the harshest of critics. I thought to myself, "Somewhere, something went array. How could a student with such low academic ability progress through the public school system for so long?" As an educator, I wondered if Nat's had been trapped in an education environment where his educational and/or social needs were unmet.

Then my thoughts drifted to Savana, another former student. Savana, much like Nat, was seventeen years old and had repeated ninth grade three times. But Savana, unlike Nat, had given up on school. She also had behavioral issues which negatively impacted her learning ability. Savana had a poor attendance record and was frequently in and out of the district Discipline Alternative Education Program (DAEP). I continued to contemplate, "how can a child with such a gleaming spirit lack the ability or even the efficacy to be successful in school?" Savana's difficulty stemmed from home and environmental instability, low-socio economic status (SES), poor school attendance, and other school related failures. To further complicate matters, Savana was also a teenage parent.

When I reviewed Savana's school records I discovered during her elementary years she was a bright student. As she entered middle school, her grades and attendance decreased and negative behavior patterns increased. By the time Savana reached high school she was waiting for an excuse to drop out.

After several years serving as principal of a nontraditional high school, Savana's story was common. Too many students were not sufficiently motivated to succeed in school.

Between Nat and Savana, Savana found inspiration and motivation in the nontraditional high school environment. She passed state assessments on the first testing, earned commended in English Language Arts and Social Studies, and graduated from high school. Savana acquired a level of self-actualization which allowed her to have a renewed commitment to rigorous learning opportunities. The Efficacious Model of Nontraditional Education approach provided the framework to capture and renew a student like Savana to soar academically. According to the theorist, Bandura (1977) through the process of differential reinforcement, successful modes of behavior are eventually selected from exploratory activities, while ineffectual ones are discarded. Bandura's notions on social learning theory forms a bridge between behaviorist and cognitive learning theory because it includes attention, behaviorist, and cognitive components. Savana is a prime example that all students have academic ability. Many students start off having it, but for some societal reasons lose it, however they can definitely regain it.

And then, there was Colton, an intellectually stimulating, artistically gifted male student. Colton was born and reared in an affluent supportive family. He never liked traditional schooling, and especially resented the mainstream high school route. Colton was never interested in extra-curricular activities, not even band, yet gifted to play bass guitar, piano, flute, saxophone, and drums. Colton often shared that he did not have the patience for his high school peers and found them to be uninteresting and immature. He dreaded the four-year high school route. In fact, he often expressed his desire to graduate early, enter college, and start the path to his career dreams.

Because of the pace at the nontraditional high school, clearly, Colton exceeded expectations. He took advantage of every academic and social opportunity, completed his high school credits, passed all state assessments, and graduated within two and a half years.

My work with students like Nat, Savana, Colton, and thousands more inspired me in my dissertation research which was "Credit-Recovery Nontraditional Alternative High Schools: An Answer to Disenfranchised Students". This book is an effort to utilize and heighten student graduates' voices and to help inspired educators to reclaim future disenfranchised, disengaged, and at-risk students.

Before beginning this research project, my review of literature, resulted in 116 references. Throughout the dissertation chapters, I will be identified as "the researcher". The review of literature represented three sections covering 17 topics related to the study of the research question. The historical overview covered three areas. The first was high school dropout statistics, identifying the characteristics which identify students who are at-risk to drop out. The second was Student and Family Characteristics related to the role of family support affecting education. It contains a conflicting finding. In the next section, Theoretical Framework, I examined student behaviors, perceptions, intrinsic and extrinsic motivation, population characteristics, past and current attitudes, beliefs, opinions, and practices (Creswell, 2008). The next stage was the opportunity to participate in a credit-recovery program, which allowed students to work individually on work they were capable of completing. The final section of the literature review entitled Current Findings comprised of 11 topics. These topics provided relevance based on Bullock (2007), the rapid growth of nontraditional alternative education programs in the 21st century was empowered by the mismatch between traditional schools' expectations and students' performance and/or behavior.

The final four topics (Cultural Relevant Leadership, Credit-Recovery Programs, Variations in Credit-Recovery Program Types, and Characteristics of Effective Credit-Recovery Programs) focused on the pedagogical techniques and identified trends related to the experiences and perceptions of curriculum, instruction, and the environment of the high school.

To repeat, this book is an effort to utilize and heighten student graduates' voices and to help inspired educators to reclaim future disenfranchised, disengaged, and at-risk students. Knowledge gained from this study may identify processes that educators can use to coordinate programs for students who have experienced multiple failures in the mainstream high school. Participants' lived experiences explored in this study may help school leaders, policy makers, teachers, staff, parents, and community partners understand the unique needs of this population.

ACKNOWLEDGMENTS

I would like to thank God for the gifts, talent, and provision that allowed me to accomplish this life-long dream.

I would like to thank and acknowledge my dissertation committee, Dr. Marlene Zipperlen, Dr. Robert Rose, and Dr. Jean Kemp, University of Mary Hardin-Baylor College of Education.

A big thank you is necessary to my committee chairperson, Dr. Marlene Zipperlen, for your continued support, unconditional love, and encouragement. You have been a life-long mentor, ally, but most of all dear friend, you are family.

To my committee members, Dr. Jean Kemp, Dr. Robert Rose, and my professors, Dr. Christine Bledsoe, Dr. Robert Novotny, Dr. Hazel Rowe, and Dr. Rudolph Lopez, Jr., thank you all for your time, wealth of experiences, and incredible knowledge that you so willingly shared with me.

Lastly, I would like to give thanks to my colleagues around the globe, thank you for your support and encouragement.

DEDICATION

This book is dedicated to those who have greatly impacted my life, lifted me up, and encouraged me through this academic milestone.

Psalms 28:7 (KJV) says, "The LORD is my strength and my shield; my heart trusted in him, and I am helped; therefore my heart greatly rejoiceth, and with my song I will praise him." This book is dedicated first and foremost to God, my Lord and Savior, for blessing me with the ability to accomplish this great endeavor.

This book is also dedicated to the historical line of educators in my family who paved the way for me and so many others, Great Grandmother Martha White, Grandmother Mamma Eula Mae Jones, Great Aunt Marie Hawkins, Great Uncle Reverend L. D. White, Great Aunt Estella Mozee, Great Aunt Myrtle (Lovie) Brown Everage, my father Maurice Jones, Aunt Odeal Buhl, and Aunt Vertie Lee Mclennan.

To my husband, Sidney, and our children, my mother, Tiny Will Jones, and my brothers and sisters, all 13 of you, thank you for your love, patience, encouragement, prayers, and willingness to see me through to the end. I pray that this adventure has been an example of the importance of education to our family and friends and will continue a family legacy that binds us together with a love for learning and sharing.

To my guardian angels, daddy Maurice Jones, and baby sister Catina Jones Ford, both in heaven, I feel your presence, see your smiles, hear your laughter, and do my best to share your loving spirits. You are with me each and every moment I breathe.

To my family, dearest friends, and colleagues, thank you for your support and prayers. I love you and treasure you.

My heart and passion remains with my students, this was for you. I hear your pleas and support your dreams. I witness your ambitions, inspired by your tenacious courage, and I marvel in your success.

THE AUTHOR

Dr. Sharon D. Jones Deloach is a notable Instructional Executive Leader. For the past 25 years, she has strategically made herself available to lead cross-functional teams and model the role of an innovator. She holds a Doctor of Education degree, EC-12 superintendent, principal, and teacher certifications. She also holds counseling certificates, a non-profit certification, and is a Future Achievement International (FAI), certified Personal Leadership Effectiveness (PLE), Trainer/Coach. She has served in roles of Education Director, Analyst, Consultant, High School Principal, Assistant Principal, At-Risk Facilitator, Post-secondary Education Counselor, Teacher, and Social Service Administrator.

Dr. Deloach earned her Doctoral of Education degree from the University of Mary Hardin-Baylor. She completed her International Studies Tour in Europe, summer 2014 – touring Belgium, Germany, France, and The Netherlands learning the Dutch Vocational & University Systems collaborating with the University of Maastricht and Zuyd University & Fontys University of Applied Sciences. Dr. Deloach earned her Masters of Education degree from the University of Mary Hardin-Baylor and Bachelor of Science degree from Texas A&M University-CC.

Dr. Deloach's achievements serving as a U.S. Department of Education, OVAE, State Scholars Initiative Educational Analyst involved implementing education programs, interventions, and policy alignments with K-16 school administrators, teachers and counselors, students and parents, institutions of higher education, business organizations, philanthropic and civic organizations, legislators, and chief state education officers across the United States.

As an Instructional Leader, she is a staunch education reformer, restructuring traditional and nontraditional schools and programs; increasing district, student, and staff performance. The central aspect of her research agenda is in finding ways to effectively support students, teachers, education and industry leaders in their learning and understanding of underrepresented and disenfranchised students and workforces applying research-based culturally relevant pedagogical strategies.

Dr. Deloach's culminating experiences in education administration and principal of a nontraditional accelerated high school ignited her passion for this research and dissertation data. Dr. Deloach has received numerous recognitions including 2014 Texas Association of Alternative Education (TAAE) School Business Partnerships Award and the Military Order of World Wars (MOWW) Educator Award for her International Studies. She is a recipient of the 2013 Texas Association of Alternative Education (TAAE) Administrator of the Year Award. In 2012 she was awarded the International Rotary Club Educator Award, and the Temple Independent School District Principal of the Year Award. During the academic year of 2010-2011 her high school campus received the Temple ISD Administrator / Campus Teacher of Excellence Awards. Her service recognitions include the 2012, 2013, 2014 1st Medical Brigade Honorary Silver Knight Military Awards, 2012 General Pete Taylor Military Coalition Nomination, 2006 Southwestern College Board Star Award of Education Excellence, 2005 Girl Scouts Blue Bonnet Chapter Woman of Distinction Award, and the 2003 Texas State House of Representatives Service in Education and Mentoring Youth Awards.

ABSTRACT

Credit-Recovery Nontraditional Alternative High Schools:
An Answer to Disenfranchised Students A Phenomenological Case Study.
Deloach, S. 2015: Dissertation, University of Mary Hardin-Baylor,
College of Education.

Keywords: : at-risk students, credit-recovery, nontraditional high school, alternative education, progressive education, dropout, disenfranchised, school choice

Many school districts across this great nation are facing serious patterns of underachievement of students who do not fit well in a mainstream educational environment. The purpose of this qualitative phenomenological research study was to explore the perceptions and experiences of graduates from a credit-recovery nontraditional alternative high school that influenced his or her graduation. Nationally, many high school students are not earning sufficient credits to remain on grade level with their freshman level cohort. These at-risk students need options with stronger incentives to obtain high school credits and meet graduation requirements.

Credit-recovery nontraditional alternative high schools involve an at-risk student population who are at a greater risk of academic, social, and emotional struggles. These students benefit from additional support that a nontraditional setting offers. This study involved interviewing 12 high school graduates who attended and graduated from a credit-recovery nontraditional alternative high school. There was a diversified group by age and other demographics representing five graduating classes. With this research study, the investigator determined graduates' perceptions of credit recovery in their nontraditional alternative high school were overwhelmingly positive. The lived experiences explored in this study may help school leaders, teachers, staff, parents, and community partners understand the unique needs of this population.

CHAPTER 1

Introduction

Each year an average of 1.2 million students drop out of school, tantamount to one student every 26 seconds (Dessoff, 2009). Scholars suggested students nationwide disengage in useful learning, which results in falling behind academically and failing to earn enough credits toward grade promotion (Merrifield, Warne, Bentsen, O'Sullivan, & Barnett, 2013). Nationally, ninth grade students earning too few credits and failing to pass to the 10th grade are at risk of dropping out (Lloyd, 2007; Rumberger, 2011), as these students are more likely to experience repeated academic frustration and failure, and display behavior problems (Gable, Bullock, & Evans, 2006). In many school districts, the traditional high school experience is simply counterproductive for some students.

Given, the previously mentioned information, educators and administrators face pressures to help students remain in school and graduate. Many are perplexed trying to re-engage students who have demonstrated frustration with school, have personal or family issues that hinder academic success, and are inconsistent in attendance. In order to re-capture students who lack sufficient credits for grade-level promotion or graduation, credit-recovery programs at nontraditional alternative high schools may be the answer to re-engage disenfranchised students who may be potential dropouts

Nature of the Problem

Earning high school course credit is the requirement leading to high school graduation. "Some students fail to graduate, because they are unsuccessful in earning the credits needed to graduate" (Allensworth & Easton, 2005, p. 1). The first year of high school is a critical transition period for students. Students who do well in the first year usually transition to continued success and go on to graduate. For other students, course failures may simply be a sign that a student has disengaged from school as the student stops participating and completing the work, which results in failing grades (Allensworth & Easton, 2005).

Rumsberger (2001) introduced two programmatic approaches to students dropping out due to academic failure and/or behavior issues.

One approach is to provide supplemental services to students within an existing school program. The second approach is to provide an alternative school program either within an existing school (school within a school) or in a separate facility (alternative school). Both approaches do not attempt to change existing institutions serving most students, but rather create alternative programs or institutions to target students who are by a set of criteria identified as at-risk of dropping out. (p. 26)

Statement of the Problem

The general problem is perennially, significant percentages of high school students do not graduate because they are behind in grade-level credits (Allensworth & Easton, 2005; Kennelly & Monrad, 2007; Rumberger, 2001). The average high school student earns an estimated 6.5 credits per year to promote to the next grade level (Texas Education Agency, 2013). When this does not occur, students require nontraditional options to motivate him or her to obtain the necessary credits for graduation in four years. As such, the traditional school setting may produce counterproductive results, given the limited success and great expense associated with it (McIntyre-Bhatty, 2008). Because of federal and state requirements, which mandate the need to educate all children appropriately, it is reasonable to expose students' "tendency for flight rather than fight in the face of disaffection" (McIntyre-Bhatty, 2008, p. 378), and offer alternative methods that can focus on earning credit based on competency of the content standards for the particular course. Credit-recovery programs, in general, have a primary focus of helping students stay in school and graduate on time. This is particularly so, as researchers revealed credit-recovery programs are continually improving chances of graduation for at-risk students more than traditional schooling, which carries the bulk of the burden for graduating all students (Steinberg & Almeida, 2008). The specific problem is most school districts do not offer credit-recovery programs that allow students to earn credits in an accelerated manner and graduate with their freshman cohort (Steinberg & Almeida, 2008). Dessoff (2009) asserts: "Credit recovery give students who have failed courses, because of failed grades or absenteeism or who have dropped out of school, a chance to recover the credit they have lost and ultimately graduate" (p. 46).

Acquiescing, Menendez (2007), stated, "alternative schools typically provide somewhat individualized curriculum and instruction designed to meet the varied need of students" (p. 19) whose needs were not met in traditional public schools. Typically, classroom instruction includes face-to-face interaction between teachers and students, but credit-recovery solutions are emerging in stand-alone nontraditional alternative high schools. Though alternative programs and schools have been in existence for many years, there is still very little consistent, wide-ranging evidence of their effectiveness or even an understanding of their characteristics; yet, many educators believe that alternative education is one important answer to meeting the needs of disenfranchised youth (Lange & Sletten, 2002).

Purpose of the Study

Students may become disengaged and disenfranchised in schools due to his or her perception of having a lack of voice and a lack of success in the traditional school settings. The purpose of this qualitative phenomenological research study was to explore the graduates' perceptions of credit-recovery nontraditional alternative high schools. The tetrad focus of this research was to explore credit-recovery students' experiences with their nontraditional alternative high school. The first is to explore Hoyle's (1998) yet valid concern that students feel powerless in the school environment, next to determine if alternative education practices foster increased achievement levels, and finally to expose those areas preventing at-risk students from being successful (Lagana-Riordan et al., 2011). Nationally, many at-risk high school students are not earning sufficient credits to remain on grade level with their freshman level cohort; consequently, they are at-risk of dropping out of school. These at-risk students need more flexible options and stronger incentives to obtain high school credits and meet graduation requirements.

Research Design and Method

Students who graduated through a credit-recovery nontraditional alternative high school, who at one time were at-risk of dropping out of school, were the focus of this research. The credit-recovery nontraditional alternative high school is located in the Central Texas area. The design centered on participants answering open-ended questions about his or her perceptions of experiences at the credit-recovery nontraditional alternative high school. Questions focused on enrollment in a credit-recovery high school, the curriculum materials, and the types of motivators and incentives involved in the credit-recovery efforts. Identifying successful practices are important to ensure consistency throughout the interviewing process (Fontana & Frey, 2005).

The design method deals with the graduates' experiences in a credit-recovery nontraditional alternative high school. According to Creswell, Hanson, Plano, and Morales (2007), the focus of all qualitative research concentrates on understanding the phenomenon explored. Therefore, information gathered from each graduates' interview served to document his or her accounts. Creswell et al. (2007) further noted that phenomenological studies do not compare experiences; rather, they describe them while presenting a dichotomy. In summary, this study emphasized "subjectivity and discovery of the essence of an experience and [to] provide a systemic and disciplined methodology for derivation of knowledge" (Moustakas, 1994, p. 45).

Background of the Problem

Evidence of the Problem

Nontraditional alternative education began in the 1960s as a reaction to the "bureaucracy and depersonalization of public education" (McKee & Conner, 2007). Two categories of alternative schools developed: those outside the public school system and those inside. Two of the most well-known examples of alternative education were the Freedom Schools, and the Freedom School Movements (Hughes-Hassell, 2008). The Freedom Schools emerged to provide high quality education to people of color – something the school's founders felt public schools did not offer. Freedom Schools were primarily community schools, often located in church basements or store fronts (Lange & Sletten, 2002). The Freedom Schools' emphasis was on individual achievement, happiness, and fulfillment as well as academic achievement. At the same time, educators inside the public school system developed alternatives.

In the 1980s and 1990s, the focus of alternative education shifted to at-risk students, specifically students who, for various reasons, were most likely to drop out of school. Further, the emphasis was on creating programs that would motivate students to stay in school and graduate. Today nontraditional alternative education programs abound both inside and outside public education (Hughes-Hassell, 2008). These programs include charter, magnet, second chance, hospital, home, and language immersion schools (Hughes-Hassell, 2008). More than 600,000 diverse children and adolescents annually attend nontraditional alternative educational programs (Gable et al., 2006), including students who have strong religious convictions, special needs, substance abuse problems, a history of truancy, or criminal involvement (Gable et al., 2006).

According to Bullock (2007), the rapid growth of nontraditional alternative education programs in the 21st century was empowered by the mismatch between traditional schools' expectations and students' performance and/or behavior. Meeting the full range of needs presented by learners is the goal of current nontraditional alternative educational programs (Rix & Twining, 2007). The focus of this study may provide evidence a supportive student environment for students who are at risk of dropping out of high school may reduce the number of students dropping out of school.

Setting/Organizational Profile

The research site is a Central Texas credit-recovery nontraditional alternative high school, in a district that resembles an urban district. This site is noted as an innovative credit-recovery nontraditional alternative high school, which transformed its educational practices establishing solid rigor in academic curriculum and instruction, social development programs, and enrollment structures to ensure the most vulnerable students have an opportunity to enroll.

The Central Texas school district began instruction on June 13, 1883. The site is within a 5A school district with a high school enrollment of less than 2,400 students. Texas Education Agency, District Type Data, 2010-2011 classifies Texas public school districts into community types using factors such as enrollment, growth in enrollment, economic status, and proximity to urban areas (Texas Education Agency, 2013). The school district is comprised of two early childhood centers (Pre-K), nine elementary schools (K-5), three middle schools (6-8), two high schools (9-12), and a discipline alternative education campus. The district serves a very diverse student body of approximately 8,900 students.The district student population is a minority-majority district, 70% socio-economic disadvantaged, and 70% receive free and/ or reduced lunch. The credit-recovery nontraditional alternative high school serves as one of the two-mentioned high schools.

The school started approximately 15 years ago as a campus within a campus to serve truancy students and those who were not experiencing academic success at the mainstream high school, as well as for students who were involved with the courts, plagued with the reputation of transgressions from years past. The campus, considered a school program within a school, was basically a dumping ground for kids who were continuous disruptions at the mainstream campus, along with providing a credit-recovery program for students behind on coursework credits and not on track to graduate with their cohort class. The school as a campus within a campus had seen many transitional periods leading to closing and reopening the program.

The school restructured as a stand-alone Alternative Education Accountability Campus (AEAC) five years ago. Ever since its redesigned structure, the credit-recovery nontraditional alternative high school has contributed to moving the districts' high school from a 2009 academically unacceptable designation to meeting standards and moving the district's high school graduation rate from 78% to 94%. For the past five years, the credit-recovery nontraditional alternative high school contributes an average of 30% of the district's annual graduating class.

The school serves students on a rotational basis and completion of credits and success on state assessments determines a students' length of stay. The length of stay ranges from 1 to 8 months. Students can earn 1 to 13 credits within the average length of stay. The school serves 100 students daily from Grades 9-12. Every attending student was behind in credits for graduation with their ninth grade cohort. The school employs 6-full time teachers (3 women and 3 men) who teach mathematics, science, English, and social studies, as well as elective courses. The school also employs 1 full-time administrator who serves as the campus principal, 1 full-time guidance counselor, 1 administrative assistant who serves as the campus secretary and registrar, 2 part-time receptionists, and 1 full-time custodian.

Research Question

The primary research question guiding this study was:

RQ1: What are the graduates' perceptions of their credit-recovery nontraditional alternative high school and how did his or her experiences influence his or her graduation?

There were five sub-questions that support the over-arching question, and these questions are:

1. What are the graduates' perceptions of their nontraditional alternative high school experience?
2. How did this experience help him or her achieve graduation?
3. How does the at-risk student's self-efficacy relate to the environment of their school?
4. What education practices foster increased achievement levels?
5. What are the graduates' perceptions toward prevention of drop-out rates?

Theoretical Framework

The chosen theoretical framework serves to examine student behaviors, perceptions, intrinsic and extrinsic motivation, population characteristics, past and current attitudes, beliefs, opinions, and practices (Creswell, 2008). As cited in De La Ossa (2005), Gregory, Pugh, and Smith (1981) found that "alternative students reported much greater satisfaction with their schooling experiences than did students in traditional schools" (p. 26). Students who participate in credit-recovery programs, earn credits, and successfully complete state assessments is declarative that learning entails more than what is determined in traditional classrooms. While Maslow's hierarchy conveys significant variables, the scaffolding theory, self-determination theory, and Bandura's theory of self-efficacy underpin this study.

Maslow's Hierarchy of Needs

Maslow hierarchy theory often presented as a pyramid with the bottom wider, representing the lowest levels of the basic human needs, and the upper point representing the need for self-actualization (Simons, Irwin, & Drinnien, 1987). Maslow's hierarchy is a critical piece when researching behaviors of students and their environment. The five basic needs embody the pyramid; physiological, safety, love, sense of belonging, and self-actualization. Maslow's hierarchy humanistic orientation to learning is evident within the social and environmental confines of these graduates' journey (Simons et al., 1987).

The Scaffolding Theory

Scaffolding theory is one of the theoretical frameworks for this study because the credit-recovery programs operate under the scaffolding theory (Yuanying, 2011). Scaffolding originated from Vygotsky's Zone of Proximal Development. Scaffolding is the assistance provided by a teacher to a student to help the student learn to do something until the point the student no longer requires the assistance. Introduction of new concepts and skills to students requires sufficient support to produce the learning (Yuanying, 2011). Credit-recovery programs are an opportunity for students to work individually with the assistance of teachers when necessary. Scaffolding assignments based on the ability of the student develops a more independent learner.

Self-Determination Theory

Self-determination theory (SDT) is a theory of motivation (Ryan & Deci, 2000). SDT is positive tendencies developing motivation, and the factors of the social environment are combative against these tendencies (Ryan & Deci, 2000). A factor of psychological needs such as competence, autonomy, and relatedness to heighten individuals' intrinsic motivation is the primary basis of SDT. SDT asserts teaching encompasses creativity, innovation, experience, and entails more than what is determined in traditional classrooms, which is necessary at both traditional and nontraditional schools.

Bandura's Theory of Self-Efficacy

Bandura's (1987) use of social learning theory suggested humans could learn new information within the domain of school by observing other humans. Students who participate in credit-recovery require self-monitoring and self-regulation; these personal standards and environmental circumstances align with the theory of self-efficacy of human behavior. This behavior is extensively motivated and regulated by the ongoing exercise of self-influence. Bandura's notions on social learning theory forms a bridge between behaviorist and cognitive learning theory because it includes attention, behaviorist, and cognitive components. According to Bandura (1977) through the process of differential reinforcement, successful modes of behavior are eventually selected from exploratory activities, while ineffectual ones are discarded.

Significance of the Study

One student every 26 seconds dropping out of school is a detriment to the future economic growth of the United States (Dessoff, 2009). The findings of this study could advance the means by which students, engaged in useful learning, remain in school earning enough credits to graduate. If the experiences at the credit-recovery nontraditional alternative high schools increase the graduation rate of at-risk students, then identifying those experiences may help others toward a pathway to graduation. In many school districts, the traditional high school experience is simply counterproductive for some students.

Knowledge gained from this study may identify processes that educators can use to coordinate programs for students who have experienced multiple failures in the mainstream high school. The lived experiences explored in this study may help school leaders, teachers, staff, parents, and community partners understand the unique needs of this population. Finally, schools leaders wanting to establish a credit-recovery system may have better insight concerning pedagogy, curriculum, and students' socio-emotional needs.

Definition of Terms

For this study, the following definitions represent the meaning of the words used in this study:

Alternative education is a public or private elementary/secondary school that addresses unmet needs of students in a regular school and provides a nontraditional education (Bullock, 2007).

At-risk is any student who exits from K-12 education before graduating through dropping out, flunking out, pushed out, or aging out of school (Watson & Gemin, 2008).

Choice schools starts with options for alternative schools and programs. Schools of Choice usually have progressive philosophies, explicitly designed to provide choices for students, parents, and teachers. Open enrollment, charter schools, private and parochial schools, for profit contract schools, approved by district boards of education, private vouchers, and publically supported vouchers are choice schools. The ultimate exercise of parent choice is the selection of home schools (Buchanan & Fox, 2008; Pipho, 2000, Raywid, 1989).

Cohort is the number of students entering Grade 9 in a specific year and completing high school four years later at the original campus in the same school district (Texas Education Agency, 2009).

Credit-recovery refers "to a student passing, and receiving credit for, a course the student previously attempted but was unsuccessful in earning academic credit towards graduation" (Watson & Gemin, 2008, p. 4).

Pedagogy is the study of education and education practice about the best way to teach (Monchinski, 2008; Ravitch & Wirth, 2007).

Scope of the Study

Creswell (2008) defined limitations as potential weaknesses or problems with the study identified by the researcher. These weaknesses are itemized and usually associated with factors related to data collections and/or analysis. Knowing the limitations is useful, particularly for replicating a study. The delimitations of the study define the boundaries of the study. A qualitative format provides rich, in-depth, relevant data through interviews.

Limitations

Creswell (2012) advised researchers to acknowledge potential limitations that could weaken a qualitative study. A limitation for this study is the potential for students' resistance or even bias in their responses.

Additionally, some of the questions may appear personal, which may prove overwhelming for participants to provide a firm accountability for the information. The participants may refuse to answer all questions, or respond half-heartily, or feel disconcerted regarding confidentiality.

Another limitation is the small sample size, which results in the findings not being generalizable to other school districts or populations. The participants should mirror the school's population, but may not since those in the study self-select to participate by responding to an invitation. Finally, researcher bias may occur due to personal involvement in credit-recovery programs. Another limitation is the small sample size, which results in the findings not being generalizable to other school districts or populations. The participants should mirror the school's population, but may not since those in the study self-select to participate by responding to an invitation. Finally, researcher bias may occur due to personal involvement in credit-recovery programs.

Delimitations

Delimitations are choices made to set the boundaries of the study (Creswell, 2003). The selection of a qualitative research design supports the goals to gain an understanding of underlying reasons, providing insights to the phenomenon, and to uncover prevalent trends in credit-recovery programs from those closest to the phenomena. Only one Central Texas school district, and one alternative school campus is the focus of this study. The participants are former students from this credit-recovery nontraditional alternative high school, and are graduates. Male and female graduates represent the participants. One-on-one interviews represent the means for data collection.

Assumptions

Many assumptions exist, such as participants will be forthright in their responses. An assumption is the interviewee can articulate clearly, what he or she wishes to say. There is an assumption that a pattern emerges from the participants' responses. It further assumed the research questions, data collection method, and study design are applicable to addressing the research problem.

Summary

A large number of students are not experiencing success in mainstream education arenas. They are failing both academically and socially. The purpose of this qualitative phenomenological research study was to explore the graduates' perceptions of credit-recovery nontraditional alternative high schools. The effect of environmental issues has a huge impact on school and student success. Conversely, Mays once asserted, "It is not your environment, it is you, the quality of your minds, the integrity of your souls and the determination of your will that will decide your future and shape your lives" (Chang & Terry 2007, p. 29). Credit-recovery programs in a nontraditional alternative school setting were the focus of this qualitative phenomenological research study.

The review of literature is the focus of Chapter 2. Historical narratives of the school system and credit-recovery programs are in Chapter 2. A detailed analysis of the theoretical framework that guided this study is also included in Chapter 2.

CHAPTER 2
Review Of Literature

Students fall behind in attaining high school course credits due to varied reasons. Consequently, those students falling behind rarely recover lost course credits resulting in remaining behind in his or her grade level. When students fail courses, fail to achieve promotion, and/or drop out of school, the result is detrimental to the student and to the school district (Dessoff, 2009). Recent researchers indicated students who attended an academic nontraditional alternative school for at-risk youth earned more credits and have higher graduation rates than their peers who continued to attend traditional schools (Streeter, Franklin, Kim, & Tripodi, 2011). Although many researchers have explored the public school characteristics helping at-risk students complete high school programs, the research on credit-recovery nontraditional alternative high schools is limited. The available research predominantly focuses on describing alternative school populations and program characteristics rather than focusing on the effectiveness of credit-recovery nontraditional alternative high schools.

In an attempt to address growing trends in education by way of choice schools and credit-recovery options, this chapter reviews literature to determine whether prejudices, biases, and stereotypes exist toward alternative education. Raywid (1989) noted three fundamental premises supported by empirical support bring about choice. One, there is no one best choice for everyone. Two, diversity in school programs and structure accommodates all students. Three, when students have the option to choose there are greater accomplishments in the learning environment and performance is better.

The purpose of this qualitative phenomenological research study was to explore the graduates' perceptions of credit-recovery nontraditional alternative high schools. Only a few researchers suggested these schools are successful in meeting the educational needs of at-risk youth (Lagana-Riordan et al., 2011).

Documentation

Documentation within the literature review focused primarily on credit-recovery, nontraditional, alternative schools, and programs. The literature researchers proved relevant yet encompassed a broader base to support credit-recovery options in nontraditional and alternative schools. There are 116 references in this study. Because credit-recovery is novel on the educational schema, there was restricted research using the coined phrase. Credit-recovery alone provided limited search opportunities. Searches of various websites and databases yielded the collection of sources. ERIC, EBSCO articles, dissertations and theses databases were useful in identifying the sources but did not provide substantial amount of research on the topic credit-recovery. Search results from google scholar and academic search complete yielded the most generous collection of sources. Google scholar provided more sources using the phrase credit-recovery.

Seventy percent (81) of the sources are less than 10 years old dating from 2004 up to 2014, and 30% (35) are older than 10 years, dates from 2003 back to 1977. There is one book dated 1938 which is about one of the most revealing theorist for transforming education. In spite of a publication date over 60 years ago, Dewey's book proved to be relevant to the credit-recovery and nontraditional educational research. Sixty-eight percent of the sources were from peer reviewed articles, 15% from professional journals, 9% from books, and 14% from government publications. The remaining sources were from dissertations, papers, presentations, and other articles. Much of the literature on credit-recovery is documented material emerging within the past five years.

Historical Overview

High School Dropout Statistics

For at least two decades, conservatives have argued that school choice is the last unachieved civil right (Scott, 2012), particularly for at-risk youth. According to the Texas Education Agency Public Education Information Management System (PEIMS), a student at risk of dropping out of school includes each student who is under 21 years of age and according to TEC §29.081, Compensatory and Accelerated Instruction 2012 -2013 may have the following characteristics:

Is in prekindergarten, kindergarten or grade 1, 2, 3, and did not perform satisfactorily on a readiness test or assessment instrument administered during the current school year; is in grade 7, 8, 9, 10, 11, or 12 and did not maintain an average equivalent to 70 on a scale of 100 in two or more subjects in the foundation curriculum during a semester in the preceding or current school year or is not maintaining such an average in two or more subjects in the foundation curriculum in the current semester; was not advanced from one grade level to the next for one or more school years; (*Note*: From 2010-2011 forward), TEC 29.081 (d-1) excludes from this criteria prekindergarten or kindergarten students who were not advanced to the next grade level as a result of a <u>documented</u> request by the student's parent; did not perform satisfactorily on an assessment instrument administered to the student under TEC Subchapter B, Chapter 39, and who has not in the previous or current school year subsequently performed on that instrument or another appropriate instrument at a level equal to at least 110 percent of the level of satisfactory performance on that instrument; is pregnant or a parent; has been placed in an alternative education program in accordance with TEC §37.006 during the preceding or current school year; has been expelled in accordance with TEC §37.007 during the preceding or current school year; is currently on parole, probation, deferred prosecution, or other conditional release; was previously reported through the Public Education Information Management System (PEIMS) to have dropped out of school; is a student of limited English proficiency, as defined by TEC §29.052; is in the custody or care of the Department of Protective and Regulatory Services or has, during the current school year, been referred to the department by a school official, officer of the juvenile court, or law enforcement official; is homeless, as defined NCLB, Title X, Part C, Section 725(2), the term "homeless children and youths", and its subsequent amendments or; resided in the preceding school year or resides in the current school year in a residential placement facility in the district, including a detention facility, substance abuse treatment facility, emergency shelter, psychiatric hospital, halfway house, or foster group home. (pp. 38-39)

The Texas Dropout Report (1994-1995) officials cited the most common reasons students in Texas leave school as: 1) poor attendance, 2) employment, 3) low or failing grades, 4) over-age for grade-level, 5) pregnancy, 6) suspension/expulsion, 7) not meeting graduation requirements, 8) marriage, 9) to attend a GED program, or 10) to enter a non- state-approved alternative program. Once students fail courses and face the prospect of repeating a year the process starts. Kronholz (2011) explained, young people fall behind when they do not attend school, and because they are so far behind in lessons and content knowledge they become disconcerted or ashamed so they stop attending which makes them further behind.

Iachini, Buettner, Anderson-Butcher, and Reno (2013), described to understand the academic disengagement and reengagement process from the perspective of students enrolled in a dropout recovery charter school. This perspective focused on students' perceptions of the factors that influenced their lack of success in the traditional school setting and the factors currently promoting their success in this new school setting. Students reported individualization of learning, school structure, and school climate as factors promoting current success.

The negative correlations associated with a lack of high school diploma are vast (Feinberg, 2004). The financial and social costs stemming from high school failure/dropout rates in the United States are enormous. Those who do not earn a high school diploma are more likely to experience unemployment and earn a lower annual wage. Added, they are more likely to experience imprisonment (Wright, 2012). In fact, for the United States to meet 21st century labor market demands, sustain a viable economy (Afterschool Alert, 2009), and earn livable wages, formal education is necessary (Franco & Patel, 2011).

Student and Family Characteristics

One often hears of first-generation college students but less often hear about first- generation high school graduates. For some families the tradition of high school graduation does not seem possible. Each first-generation high school student exponentially raises the odds and expectation of graduation rooted into subsequent children. Students who graduate as first-generation high school graduates, especially, those of the Hispanic and African-American minority ethnic groups build family traditions (Christie, 2008). Regardless of education level, ethnic background or income level, parents want their kids to be successful in school; however, they do not know how to support their children (LaRocque, Kleiman, & Darling, 2011). Family support is of major importance in predicting student achievement (Dornbusch & Ritter, 1988). Tyler and Lofstrom (2009) reported students regularly reported measures of disengagement as the primary reasons for leaving school. The commonality of responses such as "I did not like school," and "the classes were not interesting" is often cited as a reason schools must become more relevant and that teachers must learn to structure curriculum and pedagogy so that it is more interesting and engaging to students at risk of dropping out" (p. 84). These students may display fear of new challenges due to feelings of devastation caused by previous setbacks. Yet, these same students, with proper goal setting, educational techniques, and encouragement, and support from school and community can exhibit resilience and grow to relish new challenges (LaRocque et al., 2011).

Family background, socioeconomic status, and environment influences whether a student will succeed in school (Raywid, 1989). Family involvement in the students' opportunity to learn at home and at school is the parental investment of resources in their children's education (Sheldon, 2002). Families in low socioeconomic status may have fewer years of education and may have experiences that are more negative in schools. High or low levels of student academic confidence, self-esteem, greater school engagement, fewer behavior problems, greater ambitions, and lower stress are contingent on emotional support from family structure (Christenson, Rounds, & Gorney, 1992).

Family stability, reflected in both family structure and school mobility links to quitting school. Potentially important, but less well researched, are the roles played by family preferences and attitudes, and how well families are informed about the importance of education in modern society (Ellison & Trickett, 2006). Student's family background greatly affects his or her educational outcomes and is the most commonly viewed important predictor of schooling achievement. "Among the strongest family domain dropout predictors are parental education, occupation and income,-in other words socioeconomic status" (Tyler & Lofstrom, 2009, p. 85).

McNulty and Roseboro (2009) reported public schools serve distinct and competing purposes. The researchers further stated schools exist as reproductive sites—places that allow the dissemination of knowledge and processes that maintain the existing social order. Their ethnographic study was composed of observations and interviews with seventh grade students as a method to collect data. The researchers' interviews with the students resulted in identifying the students' environment. Certain environments deemed as stereotypically biased spaces based upon family achievement.

Knowing that true learning encompasses more than what is determined in a traditional classroom, the Gestalt perspective regularly incorporates creativity, innovation, experience, and experimentations (Woldt & Toman, 2005). Authenticity, optimism, holism, health, and trust are important principles to consider when approaching teaching and learning from the perspective of Gestalt theory. Like Gestalt's common themes, organismic self-regulation, learning is optimally a self-regulatory process involving the learner's whole being with self-determined boundaries and contacting processes in response to the field conditions. In agreement with Gestalt therapy theory, teaching and training (pedagogy) rely on the belief that people are by nature seeking (Woldt & Tolman, 2005). Individuals are more prone to respond positively to an *invitation to learn* than an *order* to learn. Learning from desire and internal motivational forces is far superior to mandated learning based on fear. Gestalt pedagogy, then, involves a statement of trust and belief in the inherent ability to the organism. The student knows his or her own needs and has the ability to formulate a plan of action for satisfying these needs (Woldt & Tolman, 2005).

The perception that one has the responsibility of controlling behavior, actions, and life circumstances creates a source of power. Locus of control is a theory of personality psychology referring to the extent to which individuals believe he or she can control events that affect their lives. According to Miller, Fitch, and Marshall (2003), students' locus of control or lack thereof is a top struggle in schools. Gregg (1999) and McWhirther, McWhirther, McWhirther, & McWhirther (1998) revealed three indicators of struggle leading to school failure: The first, one out of four students drop out of high school and 50% represents the drop-out rate for poor and urban high school students. Second, students and teachers have become victims of the three million crimes committed each month, and thirdly, deaths in youth related to violence have risen.

Yet each first-generation high school graduate exponentially increases the odds that, for subsequent children, the expectation of graduation will be a lock, "But locking in expectations can only happen when far greater numbers of students actually graduate--and do so fully prepared for adulthood" (Christie 2008, p. 325).

Maslow's Hierarchy of Needs

Maslow's hierarchy humanistic orientation to learning is evident within the social and environmental confines. Needs comprised of physiological, safety, love, and self-esteem are the lower level needs of survival. Rising to level five, self-actualization is the peak of the hierarchy of motivation. The inclination to actualize lies in the potential and desire for self-fulfillment. Maslow indicated education is one of the societal hindrances to personal growth, and recommended 10 response points educators should use to grow students into a self-actualized person (Simons et al., 1987).

Maslow's 10 response points supported three areas; teach, help, and refresh (Simons et al., 1987). Teaching tenets comprise authenticity by creating an awareness to hear the inner-feeling voice that connect to the inner selves; transcend trifling problems of injustice, pain, suffering, and death. Transcend to cultural conditioning allowing one to become world citizens. Teach methods to be good choosers and provide practice in making good choices along with teaching controls are good to improve the quality of life in all areas. The final being life is precious, "there is joy to be experienced in life, and if people are open to seeing the good and joyous in all kinds of situations, it makes life worth living" (Simons et al., 1987, p. 2). A discovering of a vocation based on a person's calling, fate, or destiny is what educators should do to help students find their way. This guidance will lead to finding the right career. Educators can also help by seeing that basic needs are satisfied (safety, belongingness, and esteem needs).

Maslow also suggested a refreshing of the consciousness is a position that teach appreciation of nature and its' beauty (Simons et al., 1987). Acceptance of who a person is will help the person learn their inner nature. Knowing limitations and aptitudes will build upon potentials already instilled in a person.

Theoretical Framework

The theoretical framework serves to examine student behaviors, perceptions, intrinsic and extrinsic motivation, population characteristics, past and current attitudes, beliefs, opinions, and practices (Creswell, 2008). According to De La Ossa, (2005), Gregory, Pugh, and Smith (1981) found that "alternative students reported much greater satisfaction with their schooling experiences than did students in traditional schools" (p. 26). Students, who participate in credit-recovery programs earn credits and successfully complete state assessments, accept learning as a process. While Maslow's hierarchy conveyed significant variables, the scaffolding theory and self-determination theory underpin this study.

Scaffolding Theory

Yuanying (2011) reports the original idea of

> Scaffolding comes from the work of Jerome Bruner who defines scaffolding as follows: Scaffolding is *a process* of setting up' the situation to make the child's entry easy and successful, and then gradually pulling back and handing the role to the child as he becomes skilled enough to manage it. (p. 46)

Stated differently, scaffolding is the assistance provided by a teacher to a student to help the student learn to do something until the point the student no longer requires the assistance. Scaffolding originated from Vygotsky's zone of proximal development, which describes a student's next stage in learning (Yuanying, 2011). Scaffolding theory is one of the theoretical frameworks for this study because the credit-recovery programs operate under the scaffolding theory. Credit-recovery programs allow students to work individually on work they are capable of completing. The more complex the work the teacher assists the student toward becoming a more independent learner in the concept. The teacher scaffolds the learning process by providing necessary support early in the learning process of the concept and then gradually withdraws that support until the student is able to work alone on the concept without assistance from the teacher (Bruner, 1985; Yuanying, 2011).

Self-Determination Theory

Self-determination theory (SDT) focuses more on the motivation of humans. SDT has received widespread attention in education to understand aspects associated with intrinsic and extrinsic motivation of individuals (Gagné & Deci, 2005). "It's arena is the investigation of people's inherent growth tendencies and innate psychological needs that are the basis for their self-motivation and personality integration, as well as for the conditions that foster those positive processes" (Ryan & Deci, 2000, p. 68). SDT is about the positive tendencies that develop motivation, and the factors of the social environment that are combative against these tendencies (Ryan & Deci, 2000). Investigators doing research grounded in SDT have found factors of psychological needs such as competence, autonomy, and relatedness to heighten individuals' intrinsic motivation, and if not nurtured, the result is a decrease in motivation for individuals (Gagné & Deci, 2005; Ryan & Deci 2000). Determining the impact a credit-recovery program has on the perceptions students formulate toward an alternative program, toward students' motivation to complete the academic work to persist to graduation, and toward students' belief the social environmental factors influenced his or her progress is the goal of this study (Gagné & Deci, 2005; Ryan & Deci 2000).

Bandura's Theory of Self-Efficacy

Bandura's (1977a) acknowledged through social cognitive theory the role that cognitive factors play in the regulation of an individuals' behavior. In social cognitive theory, the ongoing exercise of self-influence motivates and regulates human behavior. The main self-regulative idea operates through three principal sub-functions. These include self-monitoring of one's behavior, its determinants, and its effects;

judgment of one's behavior in relation to personal standards and environmental circumstances; and affective self-reaction. Self-regulation also encompasses the self-efficacy mechanism, which plays a central role in the exercise of personal agency by its strong impact on thought, affect, motivation, and action. The same self-regulative system is involved in moral conduct, although compared to the achievement domain. In the moral domain, the evaluative standards are more stable, the judgmental factors more varied and complex, and the affective self-reactions more intense. In the inter-actionist perspective of social cognitive theory, social factors affect the operation of the self-regulative system (Gagné & Deci, 2005; Ryan & Deci 2000).

Credit-recovery researchers indicated there is a strong link between academic coursework and self-efficacy (Desoff, 2009: Franco & Patel, 2011; Kronholz, 2011: Rix & Twining, 2007; Roblyer, 2006; Rumberger, 2011). Credit-recovery offers opportunity, enthusiasm; optimism, curiosity, and interest such as critical attributes for student motivations and student self-efficacy. In general, student motivation refers to a student's willingness, need, desire, and compulsion to participate in, and be successful in, the learning process. Students with a history of course failure usually have attitudes, behavior patterns, or other barriers that are factors in course failure. Since these students often find completing coursework challenging, high schools are finding alternatives to support students who must work independently to complete credit-recovery coursework (Pemberten, 2011).

Zimmerman, Bandura, & Martinez-Pons (1992) described students as intrinsically motivated when he or she is motivated from within. Intrinsically motivated students actively engage themselves in learning out of curiosity, interest, enjoyment, or achieving their own intellectual and personal goals (Weck, 2008). Bandura (1977b) suggested that humans could learn new information by observing other humans. Students who participate in credit-recovery require self-monitoring and self-regulation. These personal standard and environmental circumstances align with social cognitive theory human behavior. Bandura's (1977b) notions on social learning theory form a bridge between behaviorist and cognitive learning theories.

According to Pemberten (2011), students in the United States education system have always failed classes, and at one time, a certain failure rate was expected and considered part of doing business in education.

> Students needing to make up credit toward graduation, often called *credit recovery* has one or more of the characteristics of students considered to be at-risk for failing to eventually graduate from high school. Opportunities for students who struggle to catch up on credit can make a difference between graduation and dropping out of school" (Shore & Shore, 2009). (as cited in Pemberten 2011, p. 2).

Current Findings

Alternative Education as Graduation Support

Over the years, many graduation support programs became high schools. The focus of these high schools is on dropout prevention programs as an intervention and means by which to provide students with support needed to stay in school. Many transformations of alternative education have taken place throughout the years leading to various forms of graduation support.

Online K-12 education, called the new alternative, is providing students and schools with an opportunity to complete high school courses through self-pacing (Kronholz, 2011). Appearing in the mid-1990s, online K-12 education was a resource for bright students who experienced little success with mainstream accelerated classes. As time progressed, online education moved into core high school courses when districts experienced teacher shortages (math, science, foreign languages). Since that time, online education continues to move in a dozen directions (Kronholz, 2011). Many online companies have developed curriculum and instruction programs to align with state standards. These companies have become aggressively competitive and available for school districts that seek to provide alternative learning environments.

The International Association for K-12 Online Learning (iNACOL) estimated that 82% of school districts now offer at least one online course (Kronholz, 2011). Using technology as an alternative to traditional classroom instruction helps to individualize instruction and allow for scheduling flexibility. However, it also requires strategizing to maintain students' motivation and engagement, and help them develop independent learning skills, self-discipline, and technology-based communication skills. There is some initial research evidence supporting the effectiveness of utilizing technology to help students complete courses required for graduation (Cavanaugh, 2001). Currently, 32% of school districts have virtual schools where online offerings range from one class to an entire high school curriculum (Kronholz, 2011).

As districts move to programs that support alternative routes to earning credits, a primary barrier is the lack of quality data about credit-recovery programs. Franco and Patel (2011) reported interactions with three high school programs—Check & Connect, Talent Development High Schools, and Career Academics. While these three programs offered positive results, there are many programs that are unsuccessful (Franco & Patel, 2011). The time has come for practical approaches to the high school dropout issue. Unfortunately, the problem is so complex that it exceeds the boundaries of traditional thinking and produces levels of frustration that tend to be dysfunctional (Downing & Harrison, 1990). Based on their study findings, Downing and Harrison (1990) recommended further investigation including studying the effects of individual environments.

Nontraditional Alternative Education

Alternative education began in the 1960s as a reaction to the "bureaucracy and depersonalization of public education" (McKee & Conner, 2007, p. 44). The two categories of alternative schools that developed were those within the public school system and others within the private sector. As aforementioned, two of the most well-known examples of alternative education were the Freedom Schools and the Freedom School Movement. Since that time, policy makers, education leaders, and others have spent billions of dollars and countless hours on committees and promoting practices that would result in student learning improving slightly (Wolk, 2010). Nevertheless, our middle schools and high schools fail in their mission to prepare all students for the next step. Rather, school personnel create environments that result in disenfranchisement, disinterest, and thereby students dropping out.

Wolk (2010) emphasized meaningful change has to occur by way of redesigning schools to meet the needs of individual students. School reforms based on standardization and rigor have taken us in the wrong direction. Consequently, the emphasis on creating programs that motivate students to stay in school and complete their graduation requirements is a necessity to stem the graduate dropout rates (Quinn, Poirier, Faller, Gable, & Tonelson, 2006).

Today, diverse arrays of alternative education programs are available for both inside and outside public education. The reasons students choose to enroll in alternative educational settings generate a continually growing list. According to Bullock (2007), the rapid growth of alternative education programs in the 21st century is the mismatch between traditional schools' expectations and student's performance, behavior, or both. In order to redesign we must look at a holistic approach. All systems are different and there are new strategies for conducting business. In this effort to educate all children, educational leaders must create institutions that can accomplish this task. Personalization is the key, and to appreciate the power of personalizing education, one has to spend time with students. Personalization shapes virtually every aspect of a school, because standardization is the antithesis of personalization, such schools do not have a traditional core curriculum with typical academic courses and rigid schedules. Students play a significant role in designing their own curriculums, which emphasize real-world learning. Student learning reflects assessment of actual work demonstrated in portfolios, exhibitions, special projects, experiments, recitals, and performance-real accomplishments rather than abstract test scores.

Schools such as The Metropolitan Regional Career and Technical Center (MET) in Rhode Island; New Country School, a public Charter school for Grades 6-12 in Henderson, Minnesota; and the Urban Academy Laboratory High School in New York City are succeeding, usually with the most disadvantaged students (Rix & Twining, 2007). The objective is to create life-long learners, develop personal values students need to negotiate the ethical and moral dilemmas of life, and provide students with the skills to be productive workers in a rapidly changing economy and responsible citizens in a democracy. Meeting the full range of needs presented by learners is the goal of current alternative educational programs (Rix & Twining, 2007). According to Gregory, Pugh, and Smith, (2005), students from alternative schools reported a much greater satisfaction with their schooling experiences than did students from traditional schools (as cited in De La Ossa, 2005).

Social Declaration

In the 1980s, A *Nation at Risk* was the first attempt to address U.S. failing schools. During the 1990s, the *No Child Left Behind* legislation was yet another attempt. In the 2000s, alternative education became the new trend for schools to address the needs of failing mainstream schools (Sagor, 1999). Many successful models of alternative education in the form of charter schools, private schools, and public alternative education centers exist under the umbrella of school districts. These schools not only teach curriculum and practice pedagogy, but also provide guidance related to the social woes surrounding students, parents, and society (Sagor, 1999). Addressing students' views of alternative education and the views of the education community may provide a foundation for alternative education for at-risk students.

Kuykendall (2004) examined what contributes to the low success rate of many children in public schools. The author addressed Hispanics and Blacks as those who largely come from backgrounds of poverty. Kuykendall asserted the difficulties come from cultural misunderstandings and the inability to communicate across cultures. To move towards success for all students, educators must strive to truly understand cultures and communicate in ways that reach all cultural groups. The misunderstandings affecting teacher attitudes and expectations are prior achievement, prior behavior, prior placement, socioeconomic status, language ability, physical attributes, gender, and race/ethnicity. Issues of inequity and the achievement gap not only concern school environments, but also all who are interested in breaking down the barriers racism creates in both schools and society.

Kuykendall (2004) discussed the impact self-image has on a student's achievement and motivation, and describes characteristics of low academic self-image. The author concluded parents' economic and educational backgrounds, marital status, peer interaction, and other factors influence that self-image. Understanding the hidden societal rules of the poor, middle, and wealthy classes helps one understand the culture of poverty, and its impact in schools. Because schools traditionally operate under a middle class framework, knowing the rules and culture allows students from poverty to make appropriate choices for academic success. Additionally, Kuykendall (2004) asserted the majority teaching forces, which are White, must learn about and understand diverse student populations to provide culturally responsive instruction and pedagogy.

The Role of the Nontraditional Alternative School

The 1960s and 1970s were periods of unprecedented upheaval in America. In 1954, *Brown vs. Board of Education of Topeka* (1954) declared that separate was inherently unequal. The persistence of racism and segregation remained long after the 1954 *Brown vs. Board of Education* decision. The continued denials of opportunity still manifest itself in U.S. schools, profoundly in secondary schools. The failure to address long festering issues of social justice led to, among other things, an intense alienation among youth. In many communities, the manifestation of the discontent of middle class youth became as great as the society's problems. Society had only begun to address school failure issues pertaining to the poor and disenfranchised. The avalanche of youthful rebellion became a stimulus for action by concerned educators. One legacy of the period is the alternative movement. Embraced for its successes in providing safe and caring haven for youth was alternative education. The responsibility for providing free and appropriate education for all children is the law. Alternatives in the structure and function of the mainstream school implied an abandonment of what had made America stable, powerful, and prosperous. Thus, it would appear, alternative education programs served as a form of segregation for disadvantaged and alienated students. In the 1960s, alternative schools did not attract, recruit, or enroll students who were on a trajectory for success.

Characteristics of Nontraditional Alternative Schools

The term *alternative* school applies to many types of school settings (Trickett, McConahay, Phillips, & Ginter, 1985). Franklin (1992) shared many definitions and descriptions in the literature, which target emerging nontraditional schools. Despite their dissimilarity, there are definable themes about the structure and philosophy of quality alternative schools (Mottaz, 2002). Identified characteristics of effective alternative schools are small size, supportive environment, individual programming, many choices, autonomy, democratic structure, participation of family and community, well-defined standards and rules, targeted services, accountability, and constant evaluation.

Franklin (1992) maintained school programs have become more mainstream and institutionalized in the norms of the dominant school culture. The alternative schools' mission is to provide better and more effective educational strategies by implementing equity, flexibility, choice, and comprehensive services, compared to what is lacking in the mainstream public schools. According to Menendez (2007), regardless of the setting, "alternative schools typically provide somewhat individualized curriculum designed to meet the varied needs of students whose needs are not being met in traditional public school classrooms" (p. 19). Lehr, Lanners, and Lange (2003) characterized alternative schools as, student-supportive environments, with smaller classes and greater individual attention providing more opportunities.

Pipho (2000) reported the trend of parents having more choices in schooling is increasing in every manner, locality, and across every state in the nation. Pipho drew closer attention to the historical enrollment trend in choice schooling such as charter schools, voucher activity, and home schooling. Pipho addressed the phenomenon and fascination with choice schools, and the political debates surrounding state-funded vouchers and the federal role in education. This report also provided data on the boom of charter schools under President Clinton and the State of Charter Schools report in 2000. Pipho's report also included data to support positive reviews of charter schools to resource limitations. Choice is the attraction for many parents and charter schools for the reason of perception to fit certain student populations. Because of the range of choices, it is more difficult for parents to choose an education path for their students (Pipho, 2000).

A large number of students are not experiencing success in mainstream education arenas. Many students are failing academically and socially. The effect of environmental issues has a huge effect on school and student success. Mainstream education must be prepared to deal with these environmental issues. To address educating these students' more resources are necessary.

Barriers of Nontraditional Alternative Education

The rising movement of nontraditional alternative schools has significant value on breaking the cycle of inequality and inequity. Kim and Taylor (2008) cited many reasons for the movement such as school accountability pressures, preventing student dropout, and creating environments for specialized academic rigor and successes. To satisfy the need for choice and diversity (Conley, 2002), the popularity of alternative education regained its momentum in the mid-1990s in the form of public and private voucher programs, charter schools, and magnet programs. There was a focused effort to obtain students' perspectives to discover ways to provide better educational opportunities for disenfranchised and or disengaged students. This qualitative case study concentrated on the experiential knowledge of Prairie Alternative High School and closely observed its activities and phenomena (Stake, 2005). The significant findings included a caring environment for the students, which gained their trust and encouraged students to achieve their goals by providing a needed equitable education. In conclusion, Stake (2005) pointed out that as the numbers of alternative schools grow, educators must develop programs that disrupt the status quo to lead to educational policy for equality and social justice. Kim and Taylor (2008) suggested providing an alternative program that removes inequalities and disequilibrium, one must decide for whom is the education alternative. Vandeboncoeur (2009) asserted alternative education re-engages youth after exclusion from mainstream affording a space after displacement. "Embedded in the production of alternative programs are tensions that arise between a democratic ideal of public education and a neo-liberal economic rationality that maintains the sorting machine function of compulsory schooling" (Vandebonocoeur, 2009, p. 281).

Cultural Awareness

Understanding and practicing *cultural relevant pedagogy* is: "A theoretical model that addresses student achievement but also helps students to accept and affirm their cultural identity while developing critical perspectives that challenge inequities that schools perpetuate" (Ladson-Billings, 1995, p. 469). Roosevelt (1999) provided a framework needed to improve our role as leaders in a diverse world. The author explained cultural awareness is how one communicates daily, creates effective relationships within schools, communities, families, companies, and work teams. To thrive one must be willing to understand and relate to other's differences. These learning tools enhance school environments and daily living. Individuals at all organizational levels are responsible for helping to create an organization environment that works for all. It also rests on the belief that individuals, who approach school diversity with confidence and address it with skill, not only help their educational arena approach, address, and leverage diversity in areas that offer competitive advantages, but enhance personal success as well. Further, the Roosevelt (1999) stated:

> Diversity-mature individuals know that diversity is not the same as inclusion. Achieving diversity is not the same as ensuring the mixture reflects the total population of potential members. The first is about openness to differences in attitudes, perceptions, and behaviors. (p. 10)

According to Roosevelt (1999), two major types of diversity exist: attribute and behavior. Attribute diversity refers to one's ethnicity age, education, and similar demographics. Behavior diversity refers to one's behavior, which may be a function of an attribute. Roosevelt concluded people who exhibit mature characteristics of diversity demonstrate skills that induce "good judgment and wisdom" (p. 16). To negotiate an organization or work team appropriately may be the result of one who understands attribute and behavior diversity. This implies that school leaders must incorporate comprehensive faculty development with self-efficacy building activities to prepare culturally responsive teachers and, to develop confidence in their abilities to execute the practice of teaching (Siwatu, 2001). In addition, school leaders must devise ways to infuse the teacher education curriculum with scholarship of culturally responsive teaching.

Dray and Basler Wisneski (2011) declared the forefront of the education movement is to be a culturally responsive educator. Such an environment is positive and expresses how the school's environment affects all, not just the students. An environment of this nature also reduces inappropriate biases toward students, particularly those of African American descent, or other ethnic backgrounds.

Culturally Relevant Leadership

Public schools are serving a heterogeneous student population now more than ever (Riehl, 2000). Drawing on normative, empirical, and critical literatures, Riehl (2000) explored the role of school administrators in responding to the needs of diverse students. Highlighted were three administrative tasks fostering new meanings about diversity: promoting inclusive school cultures, instructional programs, and building relationships between schools and communities. Inclusive administrative practice is rooted in values of equity and social justice; it requires administrators to bring their perspectives and experiences to bear on their practices, and it implicates language as a key mechanism for both oppression and transformation. Dray and Basler Wisneski (2011) explained the culturally responsive educator understands institutions, reflects upon their own personal assumptions, and seeks to determine how their behavior and communication style nurtures the tension between educators and his or her students. Contrary to the deficit model, Dray and Basler Wisneski (2011) suggested these efforts assist teachers and administrators in remaining aware of their responses to others. School districts across the nation are facing a shortage of effective school administrators, lack of teacher and student morale, limited resources, academic failures, lack of parental involvement, and commitment. Principal leaders possess knowledge, skills, experiences, courage, and influence that will effect real, intended change. Harvey, Holland, & Hensley (2012) suggested this comes in the form of shaping, creating, and cultivating the environment to lead to improvement. Change comes through academic vision based on high standards shaping all students for success. A climate hospitable to education creates a safe cooperative spirit cultivating leadership in others. Teachers and other adults will assume responsibility in grasping and supporting the school vision. A deliberate attempt to improve instruction enables teachers to teach at their best and students to learn at their utmost. The principal remains as the central source of leadership influence managing people, data, and process to foster school improvement (Biddle & Saha, 2005; Khalifa, 2011).

Credit-Recovery Programs

Credit-recovery refers to students recovering course credits that they forfeit due to school failure or dropout (Afterschool Alert, 2009). Credit attainment refers to alternative methods of gaining credit outside of *seat time* in the classroom (Afterschool Alert, 2009). Credit-recovery programs provide an opportunity for students to earn credit for courses previously failed due to, perhaps, the aforementioned life circumstances. Some district personnel also allow students who participate in a credit-recovery program to accelerate credits by completing courses at the next grade-level. Some districts allow students to replace a failing grade once earning the credit while others do not. Still, the result is that students can earn enough credits to complete their high school course requirements toward graduation. Although, there is limited research for credit-recovery programs, it is foreseeable that students who are truant or over-aged for their grade-level *and* fall behind in acquiring credits toward graduation, are at a higher risk for dropping out than those who regularly attend school and acquire credits alongside their peers. Students at particular risk for falling behind with course credits include youth with adult responsibilities and teen mothers (Afterschool Alert, 2009); youth involved with the criminal justice system; older immigrant and English language learners; youth who regularly move from one school to another; youth with learning disabilities or emotional and behavioral issues; and youth aging out of the foster system.

Once students fall behind, it is difficult for them to get back on track within their regular school (Afterschool Alert, 2009). School days are limited, and with the responsibilities and/or circumstances previously listed, a traditional education has proven counterproductive. A relatively unique approach to help students who have failed one or more courses at the high school level is a credit-recovery program. Although details of such programs vary from district to district, the one unifying aspect for any credit-recovery program is the opportunity for students to earn credit for a course failed (Franco & Patel, 2009).

Variations in Credit-Recovery Program Types

While there are some district level credit-recovery programs, state agencies are now developing their own credit-recovery programs. Many programs, district and state, allow students to work at their own pace, while others impose a student seat time and/or student course completion time. As confirmed by Watson and Gemin (2008), freshmen who fail at least one course are four times more likely to fail to graduate in four years. Watson and Gemin shared a credit-recovery short-term goal is to help freshmen recover course credits forfeited due to failure; long-term goals were to reduce the dropout rate and ultimately contribute to a high graduation rate for freshmen cohort classes. Results revealed credit-recovery programs allowed students to recover credits, and fostered the opportunity for students to stay on track for graduation with their freshman cohort (Pemberton, 2011, Trotter, 2008, Watson & Gemin, 2008).

Credit-recovery programs may be offered via computer software, online instruction (including through a state's virtual high school or a local virtual school), or teacher-guided instruction (small group or one-on-one); they are typically targeted at the standards in which students are deficient. Most credit-recovery programs have an online component; some are more online. Dessoff (2009) reported a number of for-profit credit-recovery programs are available to school districts around the nation. Some of these programs include Apex Learning, PLATO, K!@, Telania, and Aventa Learning. Other programs such as A+ Learning courseware and Edgenuity boast of their alignment with state curriculum requirements and accreditation from state education agencies. Although the goals are the same, each program has a unique approach. Many districts rely on these programs rather than creating an online credit-recovery system unique to their district. Nevertheless, sometimes students fail to earn credit for a course because they have not performed all of the required tasks, did not consistently attend class, and/or got crossways with the teacher. Credit-recovery is "one means of making up for prior bad decisions" (Zinth, 2011, p. 2). Credit-recovery programs help at-risk students meet promotional requirements because of the e-learning aspect of credit-recovery, which in turn has helped changed students attitudes about credit-recovery (Washburn, 2004).

Many educators are turning to afterschool programs to reach students who are at-risk of dropping out or have already dropped out (Afterschool Alert, 2009). Afterschool provides older youth with critical academic supports including credit-recovery and credit attainment. These programs are more engaging for older youth because of the provisions made to engage their interests and passions (Afterschool Alert, 2009). Franco and Patel (2011) reported, "The use of credit-recovery programs has been on the rise" (p. 19). Since the mid-1990s, over half of states in the U.S. have developed credit-recovery programs (Blomeyer, 2002; Roblyer, 2006; Watson, 2005).

According to the Education Commission of the States (2011), little to no research is available on the effectiveness of credit-recovery programs, perhaps because the option is relatively low. However, Texas dropout recovery efforts use online credit-recovery among its approaches and demonstrated results. A 2010 report of the Texas Dropout Recovery Pilot Program (TDRPP) noted that between August 2008 to May 2010, 4,141 former dropouts had enrolled in the TDRPP, of these former dropouts, 31% achieved their stated goal of either earning a high school diploma or college readiness, while 33% were continuing in the program. Just over one in three participants (36%) had left the program before earning a high school diploma or achieving college-readiness goals. While the credit-recovery component of TDRPP is not the sole factor in aiding these students toward their educational goals, this report suggests that credit-recovery shows potential benefit for contributing to the flexibility that older students, who may be a working parent, need to earn a high school diploma or achieve college-readiness goals (Education Commission of the States, 2011).

As with blended learning models, quality and accountability are important, and states should consider elements that reflect it. Determining which elements ensure that credit-recovery programs are of high quality is a suggested research topic by the Education Commission of the States (2011). According to Zehr (2010), online credit-recovery programs help districts meet the graduation demands of state and federal accountability systems, given they do not focus on hours in a classroom, but rather focus on academic proficiency.

Characteristics of Effective Credit-Recovery Programs

Scholars conducted considerable research detailing the characteristics of effective dropout prevention programs (D'Angelo & Zemanick, 2009; Trautman & Lawrence, 2004). Woods' (2002) summarized the research in five categories (as cited in Trautman & Lawrence, 2004). The first category, organization and administration, is the schools' functionality and organizational structure. Woods shared effective dropout prevention programs form smaller learning communities, maintain a low student-teacher ratio, utilize fair but uncompromising discipline strategies, are flexible in their delivery and schedule, and are particularly meticulous in their staff selection and development (as cited in Trautman & Lawrence, 2004). The second category addresses school climate, and asserts the most effective programs are orderly, and foster a family atmosphere. The third characteristic of an effective dropout prevention program is a student-centered instructional delivery method that emphasizes academic intervention, tutoring and mentoring, technology, and clear instructional objectives. Conversely, the fourth characteristic is a curriculum that allows for experiential learning, remediation, and building student self-esteem. Finally, one must consider the culture of the teaching staff. Effective choices schools employ staff who, are committed to the program's success, impose high student expectations, teach the *whole child*, and nurture a family atmosphere (Raywid, 1989).

Conclusion

While the public education system may appear to be broken, it is not; history may provide evidence it is outdated and obsolete. Dewey (1938) wrote about this same type of educational system more than 75 years ago which he termed *traditional education*. Dewey wrote about how new education, *progressive education*, began from discontent with traditional education. In progressive education, the main purpose of instruction and discipline was to prepare students to be successful citizens in a democratic society by adjusting instruction to incorporate the experiences of students. If Dewey addressed these issues approximately 75 years ago, it remains puzzling why the educational system remains characterized by the descriptions included in Dewey's (1938) book. Dewey promoted the construction of knowledge and meaning in the mind of the learner. Problem-based learning, case studies, themes, service learning, and project-based learning all describe performance learning classroom activities.

Wright (2012) emphasized a new public education system design and implementation demands inclusiveness to meet the needs of today's criteria of success for all students. Wright's study demonstrates how credit-recovery provides an alternative that is in the forefront of restructuring public education. The new public education system requires a design and implementation to meet the needs of this century and to gain buy-in from the federal and state governments, the community at-large, and school administrators. The problems facing school districts are mandates, federal requirements, lack of funding, teacher and administrator tenure, and more importantly new approaches to the organization of teaching and learning (Nicic, Petrovic, Sehovic, & Hajrovic, 2013).

Summary

The review of literature indicated there is an urgent choice for non-traditional options. Credit-recovery is a model of new methods of modernizing the educational process of cooperative learning. America must find a way to raise educational achievement in all areas for all students. "American public education needs a complete restructuring in order to support the development of critical thinkers ready to assume their positions as productive citizens of a free society" (Wright, 2012, p. 1). According to Wright (2012), providing a public education makeover can alleviate the average 30-40% dropout rate, especially in an urban center.

Developing a model high school that meets the needs of 21st century students and beyond is a credit-recovery nontraditional alternative high school with programming that emerges to provide venues and programs to prepare each student to contribute to an ever-changing, interdependent society. This review of literature is indicative that credit-recovery options provide a needs-satisfying environment where everyone can produce successfully, with the understanding that learning adds to quality of life by enabling all students to complete their high school diploma, prepare for college, and become quality workers and productive citizens. This review also revealed credit-recovery programs can improve by high margins the high school completion rate by providing differentiated instruction, improving student attendance and behavior patterns, and improving overall student performance on state assessments. Credit-recovery utilizes all outreach opportunities to ensure educational stakeholders are aware of program offerings through opportunities to participate, nurture, and actively seek new partnerships.

Almeida, Steinberg, Santos, and Le (2010) launched six pillars to effective dropout prevention and recovery to help state policymakers improve outcomes for dropouts and struggling learners.

1. Reinforce the right to a public education: States should ensure that schools and districts deliver on the federal promise that every student has the right to a free public education through high school graduation. Only raising the compulsory attendance age is not enough.

2. Count and Account for Dropouts: States should set public goals for making substantial improvements in graduation rates and use a cohort methodology to report publicly on progress toward those goals. Graduation rates, in tandem with student academic achievement, should be a key measure of accountability for districts and schools.

3. Use graduation and on-track rates to trigger significant and transformative programs: States should use new predictive indicators to ensure that individual students get the supports they need to stay in school and advance academically from the earliest signs that they are off track to earning a high school diploma. States must not neglect the more transformative strategies. They should help districts with low graduation rates implement far-reaching reforms, including the redesign of high schools losing the most students and the implementation of new models to accelerate student learning and get off-track students back on track to a high school diploma and

postsecondary attainment difference in the economic prospects of their youth.

4. Invent new models: States should create and sustain a designated vehicle for developing and implementing back-on-track models, using competitive grants and other such funding mechanisms to encourage continuing innovation and the expansion of successful models.

5. Accelerate preparation for postsecondary success: States should explicitly include off-track students in their strategies for accelerating high school completion and preparation for postsecondary success. Policies should encourage districts to use proven approaches (e.g., dual enrollment, online courses) to help at-risk students recover lost ground efficiently and develop the academic skills and behaviors required for earning postsecondary credentials.

6. Provide stable funding for systematic reform: States should commit stable funding to the development of dropout prevention and recovery options that effect systemic change and support the statewide expansions of successful models. (Almeida et al., 2010, pp. 2-3)

Almeida et al. (2010) reported growing recognition that dropouts and off-track students benefit from acceleration, not remediation. Credit-recovery nontraditional alternative high schools' models re-engage off-track youth and get high school students back on track for a college-ready high school diploma.

Unfortunately, funding continues to be a significant barrier. States have moved faster to identify the scope of the dropout problem rather than to appropriate enough money to sustain the programs needed to address the crisis. In addition, over the past decades, alarm over startlingly low graduation rates from large urban cities to single-high-school towns spurred several encouraging developments. These developments include better data collection and analysis, promising research into risk factors which shows that a small set of school-based variables are highly effective in predicting future dropouts, and the creation of cutting-edge prevention and recovery strategies in cities with the highest concentrations of dropouts (Balfanz, Almeida, Steinberg, Santos, & Fox,. 2009).

The referral process at-risk students experience before entering alternative school may result in less choice for the student than otherwise assumed. Atkins (2008) concluded choice depends mostly on local policies, and is therefore often unavailable. Riehl (2000) reported it is the principal's role to create inclusive schools for diverse students. An inclusive administrative practice is rooted in values of equity and social justice as a response to the needs of diverse students. This literature review covered the need for an alternative practice without prejudice or biases as achievement levels improve when educational leaders make the education system fit the needs of all children.

In Chapter 3, an explanation of the research methods and procedures used in this study occurs. The information includes participant selection methods and their organizational profiles. In addition, there are details about the survey instrument as well as procedures for data collection and analysis. t of Chapter 3.

CHAPTER 3
Methodology

The purpose of this phenomenological research study was to explore the graduates' perceptions of credit-recovery nontraditional alternative high schools. The focus of this study was to explore the experiences of students who graduated from a credit-recovery nontraditional alternative high school. This chapter contains the design of the study. Other information regards the participants in the study, the survey instrument, data collection process, and an explanation of the analysis of the data.

Research Method, Purpose, and Design

This study was a phenomenological research study. The phenomenological design is not an attempt to solve a problem, but rather to explore the experiences of students in a credit-recovery nontraditional alternative high school credit-recovery program. Since exploration is fundamental, the subjectivity gathered from a 10-question student interview questionnaire may contribute more to revealing the effectiveness of credit-recovery programs as perceived by the graduates interviewed.

With the grounded theory design selection, the researcher explored the commonalities among individuals (at-risk credit recovering students) in relation to credit-recovery nontraditional alternative high school experiences. An ethnographic design allows the researcher to examine customs and ways of life with the aim of describing and interpreting cultural patterns. The narrative choice gave the researcher the opportunity to explore a central phenomenon, which was the best approach to survey the perceptions these graduates have about their experiences at a credit-recovery school. The narrative choice also permitted the participants to share their stories about their journey to graduation.

The goal of the researcher was to determine how effective credit-recovery programs are for students who are not on track to graduate high school with their cohort class. Using the phenomenological design allowed the researcher to accomplish this goal by asking the students who graduated from a credit-recovery nontraditional alternative high school to respond to structured but open-ended questions. Using the information provided by the graduates may help policy makers and practitioners as they guide the creation of credit-recovery programs in high schools across the nation.

In this qualitative study, the concentration was on experiential knowledge of students who graduated from a Central Texas ISD credit-recovery nontraditional alternative high school where they experienced and closely observed its activities and phenomenon (Stake, 2005). An open-ended interview questionnaire was the instrument that generated the student responses. This interview questionnaire was a series of pre-established questions that all the participants received (Fontana & Frey, 2005). An analysis of the graduate responses occurred.

With the research and design method of the study, the investigator explored graduate experiences in a credit-recovery nontraditional alternative high school. All participants started high school with a freshman cohort class but none of the participants was on track to graduate high school with their ninth grade graduation cohort. Survey questions targeted the time the student got behind in credits, the point in time the participant recognized they were not on track to graduate in four years, and their experiences in the credit-recovery process. According to Creswell (2008), the focus of all qualitative research needs to be on understanding the phenomenon explored. Therefore, information gathered from the interview questionnaire documents the accounts. Creswell noted phenomenological studies are those in which individuals describe their experiences. Moustakas (1994) spoke to several approaches to analyzing phenomenological data and stated the phenomenology emphasizes subjectivity and discovery of the essences of experience and provides a systematic and disciplined methodology for derivation of knowledge.

Participants Profile

The participants were graduates from a credit-recovery nontraditional alternative high school in the Central Texas area. The criteria for selection and/or exclusion was the participant must have attended the Central Texas nontraditional credit-recovery alternative high school study site, must be a graduate of the Central Texas credit-recovery nontraditional alternative high school study site, and must be at least 18 years of age to participate in the study.

While attending the Central Texas credit-recovery nontraditional alternative high school, all participants were coded as at-risk based on Public Education Information Management System (PEIMS), and the standards are located in TEC 29.08 (Texas Education Agency, 2013). While these graduates were at-risk when they were students, they are no longer associated with the school district, and are young adults between the ages of 18-23. Participation in this study was voluntary. Participants were free to withdraw from this study at any time without any negative consequences by advising the researcher. There were 12 participants in the research study. Of the 12 participants, the first two who responded with a yes to participate served in the pilot study used to validate the survey instrument.

Setting or Organizational Profile

The research site was a Central Texas credit-recovery nontraditional alternative high school, in a small district that resembles an urban district. This site is notable as an innovative credit-recovery nontraditional alternative high school alternative, which transformed its educational practices establishing solid rigor in academic curriculum and instruction, social development programs, and enrollment structures to ensure the most vulnerable students have an opportunity to enroll.

The Central Texas school district began instruction on June 13, 1883. The site is within a 5A school district with a high school enrollment of less than 2,400 students. Texas Education Agency, District Type Data, 2010-2011 classifies Texas public school districts into community types using factors such as enrollment, growth in enrollment, economic status, and proximity to urban areas (Texas Education Agency, 2013). The school district is comprised of two early childhood centers (Pre-K), nine elementary schools (K-5), three middle schools (6-8), two high schools (9-12), and a discipline alternative education campus. It serves a very diverse student body of approximately 8,900 students. The district student population is a minority-majority district, 70% socio-economic disadvantaged, and 70% receive free and/or reduced lunch. The credit-recovery nontraditional alternative high school serves as one of the two-mentioned high schools.

The school started approximately 15 years ago as a campus within a campus to serve truancy students and those who were not experiencing academic success at the mainstream high school, as well as for students who were involved with the courts and plagued with the reputation of transgressions from years past. The campus, considered a school program within a school, was basically a dumping ground for kids who were continuous disruptions at the mainstream campus, along with providing a credit-recovery program for students behind on coursework credits and not on track to graduate with their cohort class. The school as a campus within a campus had seen many transitional periods leading to closing and reopening the program.

The school was restructured as a stand-alone Alternative Education Accountability Campus (AEAC) five years ago. Ever since its redesigned structure, the credit-recovery nontraditional alternative high school has contributed to moving the districts' high school from a 2009 academically unacceptable designation to meeting standards and moving the district's high school graduation rate from 78% to 94%. For the past five years, the credit-recovery nontraditional alternative high school contributes an average of 30% of the district's annual graduating class.

The school serves students on a rotational basis and completion of credits and success on state assessments determines a students' length of stay. The length of stay ranges from 1 to 8 months. Students can earn 1 to 13 credits within the average length of stay. The school serves 100 students daily from Grades 9-12. Every attending student was behind in credits for graduation with their ninth grade cohort. The school employs 6-full time teachers (3 women and 3 men) who teach mathematics, science, English, and social studies, as well as elective courses. The school also employs 1 full- time administrator who serves as the campus principal, 1 full-time guidance counselor, 1 administrative assistant who serves as the campus secretary and registrar, 2 part-time receptionists, and 1 full-time custodian.

Population Demographics

Purposeful sampling was best suited for this qualitative research study because it provided the participants needed who have experienced the value of a credit-recovery nontraditional alternative high school (Creswell, 2012). This purposeful sampling method generated homogenous sampling of students who graduated from the same credit-recovery nontraditional alternative high school (Creswell, 2012).

The 12 participants comprised the population to provide the depth of analysis necessary to contribute to decisions regarding a credit-recovery programs for students who are behind on grade-level credits. Twelve participants enabled data saturation.

Participant Selection Method

Prior to conducting the student survey, Institutional Review Board (IRB) approval was necessary. "An Institutional Review Board is a committee made up of faculty members who review and approve research so the researcher protects the rights of the participants" (Creswell, 2005, p. 151). The IRB process begins by reviewing a description of the project, proposing the informed consent form, and having the project reviewed (Creswell 2012). A major function of the IRB is to ensure participants are willing to participate and are aware of the risks associated with the study. All participants were aware of the minimal risk in participating.

According to Creswell (2012), in qualitative research, the participants for purposeful sampling are based on places and people that can best help understand the central phenomenon. The central phenomenon in this study are students not earning sufficient credits to remain on grade level with their freshman level cohort and are at-risk of dropping out. Participant selection included the students who attended and graduated from the same credit-recovery nontraditional alternative high school. Since participants attending this school had not earned credits to promote to the next grade level, all were behind in credits and not on track to graduate with their freshman cohort. The criteria for eligibility to apply to this credit-recovery nontraditional alternative high school is the student must be behind the cohort group by a minimum of three credits.

An open records request for the names of the graduates from the credit-recovery nontraditional alternative high school in the Central Texas Area was made at the district office of Student Services. Of the possible 600 graduates, the list was randomized to 60 by taking every 10 graduates. The list was further reduced to 30 by taking every other name. Those 30 received an invitation to participate in the study by letter and/or email or phone communication from the researcher. The first 12 graduates responding to the letter, email, or verbal yes in a phone conservation were study participants. The first two graduates to respond with yes to participate served in the pilot study. The next 10 consenting were the study participants. This study did not require parent consent since the graduates are 18 years-of-age.

The average amount of credits students were behind when applied was 15 credits, the average age of students were 17 years old, and their grade was ninth grade (most students were three time ninth graders). Therefore, as Creswell (2012) suggested selection of people or sites who can best help one understand the phenomenon is a purposeful qualitative sampling.

Research Instrument

The instrument for the study consisted of 10 open-ended questions presented in an interview format. This interview questionnaire was the data collection instrument in this study. The researcher recorded the interviews using a digital recorder. The researcher on occasion took field notes as necessary when a statement may have an impact on the research study. The qualitative method of research explored the open-ended approach and phenomena of the graduates perceptions and experiences of credit-recovery.

According to Creswell (2012), an instrument measures the variables and if one is not available in the literature or commercially there is an option to develop your own instrument. The interview questions were not adapted from previous research. As Creswell (2012) suggested, the instrument had to be identified utilizing the phases consisting of planning, constructing, evaluating, and checking to see if the questions work. The survey instrument questions underwent a review by a panel of experts in the field of education prior to the pilot study.

Pilot Study

A pilot study, vetting the interview questions and process, supports the appropriateness and clarity of the questions. The piloting process provides compelling information to the coherence of the interview questions in relation to the central research question (Ritche & Lewis, 2003). As Creswell (2012) suggested, the instrument had to be identified utilizing the phases consisting of planning, constructing, evaluating, and checking to see if the questions work. The pilot study conducted served as a tool to determine if the participants would understand the questions as expected. The complete interview questionnaire consisted of 10 opened-ended questions targeting student experiences with credit-recovery. The interviews with the participants were one-on-one. The location of the interviews was mutual consent of both the former student and the interviewer. Using a panel of experts allowed the researcher to gain valuable feedback from a group of people in a similar professional capacity, and the piloting of the instrument with two participants validated the instrument (Creswell, 2012). In addition, Creswell (2012) noted a pilot study ensures the questions are understandable and meet the interview protocol. The results of a pilot study determine the validity of the instrument.

Interviewing participants had both advantages and disadvantages. The advantages of interviewing include gaining first-hand information otherwise not gained in an observation or document exploration (Creswell, 2012). A clear disadvantage in the interview process as noted by Creswell (2012) includes the interviewees responding to questions with regard to pleasing the interviewer rather than answering the question completely. Consequently, the phenomenological design demands the interviewer to have a strong command of linguistics and encourages the interviewees to provide vivid recanting in order for the researcher to gain the participants lived experiences (Giorgi, 2012).

Procedures for Data Collection

One-on-one interviews with 12 former students from the Central Texas area who are graduates from a credit-recovery program provided the data. The interview process allowed the participant to describe his or her experience in his or her own words (Hayes & Singh, 2012).

The expectations are the participants gave a full description of their experiences and their thoughts, feelings and reactions to the experiences. Open-ended interview questions comprised the process designed to address the central research question: What are the graduate's perceptions of their credit-recovery nontraditional alternative high school and how did his or her experiences influence his or her graduation?

During the interview, audiotaping of open-ended interview questions and answers occurs. In addition to the audiotaping, the interviewer created notes and documentation of each interview. Each interview took 30-45 minutes. Since former students are 18 years old or older, parental permission was not necessary; however, the researcher notified the participants' parents. To maintain the reliability and validity of the data, each student received the same survey questions. The same questions allow for triangulation of data so that corroborating evidence from different individuals and relative literature occurred.

Procedure for Data Analysis

The purpose of this qualitative phenomenological research study was to explore the graduates' perceptions of credit-recovery nontraditional alternative high schools. The tetrad purpose was to explore credit-recovery graduates' experiences with their credit-recovery nontraditional alternative high school. The second focused on Hoyle's (1998) problematic yet valid concern that students feel powerless in the school environment, and third, determine if alternative education practices foster increased achievement levels. Themes formulate a common idea and express in narrative form the participants lived experience (Creswell, 2013). The focus of the study may expose those areas preventing at-risk students from being successful (Lagana-Riordan et al., 2011).

The qualitative method in this study allowed the researcher to explore the open-ended approach and phenomena of the graduates perceptions and experiences of credit-recovery. All audio and paper based files generated during this study were in a locked box throughout the duration of the study. At the completion of the transcription process, each participant received a copy for member checking. Member checking validates and checks for accuracy the transcription by the interviewee and supports saturation. Member checking allows the participants an opportunity to verify the accuracy of his or her commentary (Creswell, 2012). Once all participants return the approve transcription, the researcher and the co-rater work independently reviewing the data looking for common words, emerging themes, and ideas (Creswell (2012).

Analyzing the data resulted in emerging themes, the researcher and co-rater reached consensus on minor and major themes. The themes were categorized using a hierarchical tree diagram. A tree diagram signifies a clear delineation of broad themes and narrow themes, which helps to classify the information appropriately (Creswell, 2012). The researcher analyzed the data using a co-rater to compare results and validate the findings for each interview question. After analysis, the researcher and co-rater developed primary, secondary, and tertiary themes. Each participant received a copy of his or her transcription to determine if the document reflected what he/she said. This process allowed the participants to confirm, deny, or elaborate on their responses.

The transcriber was the only person to hear the tape in addition to the co-rater. The transcriber was required to sign a nondisclosure form before gaining access to the recordings. The co-rater decreased the likelihood presuppositions influenced the interpretation of the data. Additionally, the co-rater was required to sign a nondisclosure form before gaining access to the transcript. Once data analysis began, the co-rater and researcher reviewed hard copies of the transcripts. After examination of the data, an exploration of ideas, segments, and redundancy requires analysis (Creswell, 2012). As themes emerged, the researcher and co-rater reached consensus and divide the categories of data into minor and major themes. Themes formulate a common idea and express in narrative form the participants lived experience (Creswell, 2013).

The data coding process consisted of categorizing data into general themes, then segmenting and labeling codes so that it is meaningful. All repetitious data was put together into general themes so the result is a fewer number of themes. There was no specific process for coding data, but Tesch (1990) and Creswell (2008) recommended the following steps:

1. Read the transcriptions carefully to get an understanding of the information, and record brief marginal notes of important recollections.

2. Select an observation or interview one at a time. Read the information to determine what the participant is saying. Record the meaning in the margin in no more than three words and box it.

3. Initial the coding process. Find text segments, bracket them, and assign a phrase or code word that describes the meaning of the text segment. Text segments are sentences or paragraphs that mirror a single code.

4. Code a full text and list every code word. Similar codes fall into similar groups; be aware of repetitious codes. Reduce the code list to a workable caseload of 25 to 30 to avoid over coding.

5. Use this list and return to the data. Check for new emerging codes. Look for supporting participants' quotes and circle them.

6. Take all codes and reduce them to five to seven descriptions or themes of the participants or setting. The themes are common codes combined to form major concepts. The themes will emerge from the frequency the participants discussed them during the phenomenon exploration.

Summary

Students at-risk are in danger of dropping out or have already dropped out of school. They are the focus of this study. Re-engaging students who lack sufficient amount of credits for grade levels and are behind on credits towards graduation is a concern. Another issue in dropping out of school is students who have experienced personal, family, or other issues that hindered academic success and/or attendance in the traditional school setting. Alternative education is an emerging trend in 21st century learning and many of today's youth thrive in these educational settings.

The issue of lost credits during the early years of high school and the opportunity to re-earn credits is critical to the future success of students and their ability to graduate from high school. The misunderstanding and/or labeling a nontraditional alternative education as less productive and less meaningful requires more research. These misconceptions are evident in the education community; however, this nontraditional school may prove to be the type of schools that potential dropouts may thrive in.

As students enter high school and fail courses preventing promotion to the next grade, disengagement sets in. Although there are many reasons why students fail courses, the explosion of alternative options for students to re-earn credits lost in earlier years are significantly trending upward. This body of literature not only demonstrated a strong correlation between the lack of earning high school course credits and the increased drop-out rates but also indicated a strong correlation of credit-recovery earning options decreasing the number of drop-outs.

Credit-recovery alternative schools emerged in response to a belief the public education system was not serving all students in a fair and equitable manner. Those who created alternative schools established them on the premise that students require different avenues for learning, and that alternatives were necessary to reach the vast array of students in American education" (Lehr, Moreau, Lange, & Lanners, 2004). This qualitative phenomenological study may provide meaningful contributions to the body of knowledge of credit–recovery options as a positive impact on increasing rates of at-risk high school students who recovered and accelerated credits earning a high school diploma.

Considering the distinct lack of research and written academic literature concerning credit-recovery pedagogy, the creation of credit-recovery alternative schools, and programs for many different reasons could prove monumental. "Alternative schools and programs have become recognized largely for their mission to educate students who are most at risk of failing in the regular public education system" (Lehr et al., 2004, p. 4). The results of the current study offer education administrators, school districts, and educational policy influencers access to data, which identify predictors that may result in a change of educational practices.

Chapter 3 contained a detailed description of the study, the research design, and description of the participants, school setting, and organizational profile to gather the effectiveness of credit-recovery programs in a credit-recovery nontraditional alternative high school based on experiences of students. The study findings are in Chapter 4.

CHAPTER 4
Analysis Of Data

The purpose of this qualitative phenomenological research study was to explore the graduates' perceptions of credit-recovery nontraditional alternative high schools. The focus of the study had a four-pronged approach. The tetrad included an exploration of credit-recovery graduates' experiences with their credit-recovery nontraditional alternative high school. The second included a focus on Hoyle's (1998) concern that students feel powerless in the school environment. The third was to determine if alternative education practices foster increased achievement levels, and finally to determine those areas preventing at-risk students from being successful (Lagana-Riordan et al., 2011).

Nationally, many high school students are not earning sufficient credits to remain on grade level with their freshman level cohort; consequently, they are at-risk of dropping out of school. These at-risk students need options with stronger incentives to obtain high school credits and meet graduation requirements. Credit-recovery nontraditional alternative high schools include the at-risk student population who are at a greater risk of having academic, social, and emotional issues. These students may benefit from additional support in a credit-recovery nontraditional alternative high school setting.

The first 12 high school graduates who agreed to participate in the study and had attended and graduated from a credit-recovery nontraditional alternative high school located in Central Texas represented the purposeful sampling for this qualitative study. The content of this document does not reflect any position or expression of the independent school district, the Board of Trustees, or district administration of the study site. Participants responded to the same questions, which gave the researcher an opportunity to analyze the participants' perspectives about the phenomenon of not earning sufficient credits to remain on grade level with their freshman level cohort and at-risk of not graduating.

Research Question

After interviewing the 12 graduates, the responses helped to answer the primary research question that guided this study. RQ1: What are the graduate's perceptions of their credit-recovery nontraditional alternative high school and how did his or her experiences influence his or her graduation?

There are five sub-questions that support the over-arching question, and these questions are:

1. What are the graduates' perceptions of their credit-recovery nontraditional alternative high school experience?
2. How did this experience help him or her achieve graduation?
3. How does the at-risk student's self-efficacy relate to the environment of their school?
4. What education practices foster increase achievement levels?
5. What are the graduates' perceptions toward prevention of dropout rates?

Chapter 4 contains an analysis of the 12 interviews with graduates who were students at a credit-recovery nontraditional alternative high school in a Central Texas independent school district. Data analysis consisted of identifying common themes generated from participants' interviews and correlation of participant input from the study questions. The details of the findings from the interviews and the demographics are in Chapter 4.

Demographic Characteristics of Participants

The study consisted of 12 participants comprised of male and female volunteers who graduated from the credit-recovery nontraditional alternative high school in the Central Texas area. While attending the

Central Texas nontraditional credit-recovery alternative high school, all participants' codes on Public Education Information Management System (PEIMS) were at-risk, the standards for at-risk are located in TEC 29.08. While considered at-risk when they were students, they are now young adults.

The participants in this study had to be at least18 years old, and the actual age range of the participants was 18 to 23. Of the 12 participants, six were males (2 Hispanic, 2 African-American, 1 mixed race of African-American and Caucasian, 1 Caucasian) and six were females (2 Hispanic, 3 African-American, 1 Caucasian). All participants except one have full-time employment. Seven of the participants had jobs while attending the credit-recovery nontraditional alternative high school. One graduate is a full-time nursing student and four currently attend college part-time at the local community college. Three of the 12 earned college hours. Six of the participants are parents. Of the six parents, four were parenting students while attending the credit-recovery nontraditional alternative high school.

The researcher made an open records request for the names of the 2010 through 2014 graduates from the credit-recovery nontraditional alternative high school in the Central Texas area at the district office of Student Services. Randomization of the initial list of 600 graduates helped reduce the number to 60 by choosing every 10 graduates. A further reduction to 30 occurred by choosing every other name. Those 30 selected received an invitation to participate in the study by letter and/or email or phone communication from the researcher. The first 12 participants to respond to the letter, email, or verbal yes in a phone conversation participated in the study. Each participant received an explanation about the study, the instruction for the interview, reviewed the questions, and reviewed the consent form. Prior to the interview, each participant signed the consent form. All 12 of the participants completed the study.

Pilot Study Findings

After creating the interview questionnaire, and before conducting the pilot study, a panel of experts reviewed the 10 interview questions. The panel of experts consisted of three doctoral students, three professors, and two credit-recovery nontraditional alternative high school teachers. There were a few modifications to enhance clarity including the addition of prompts and probing questions to increase open-ended responses. Once the panel agreed on the wording of the questions, the pilot study was an opportunity to ensure understand-ability of the interview questions before conducting interviews with the actual participants (Creswell, 2012). The pilot participants were the first two graduates who responded to the invitation to participate. The participants consisted of one female and one male age 20 and 23 respectively. They were African-Americans. Both participants lost credits early in their high school career and were not on track to grad-uate with their freshman cohort class. Both participants were eager to share their high school experiences and influences. The pilot study participants expressed gratitude for an opportunity to earn a high school diploma through the credit-recovery nontraditional alternative high school. The two participants in the pilot student encountered no issues regarding the clarity of the questions, therefore their data contributed to the overall findings. The first participant from the pi-lot study was an African-American female. She was a parenting stu-dent with one child while, a full-time employee, and attended college part-time. She attended her first year of high school at a mainstream high school outside of the study's Central Texas school district. She transferred into the Central Texas school district's mainstream high school as a repeat ninth grader and transferred into the credit-recovery nontraditional alternative high school as an 18-year-old 10th grader. The second participant from the pilot study was an African-American male, full-time employed licensed barber and sole proprietor of a bar-bershop. He attended his first year at the study's Central Texas school district, dropped out his 10th grade year at the age of 17, and went on to spend two years in juvenile detention center. He directly trans-ferred into the study's Central Texas school district credit-recovery nontraditional alternative high school as a 20-year-old 10th grader.

The pilot study occurred at an agreed venue and both participants appeared comfortable in their chosen setting. With participants' per-mission, the interviews were audio recorded to facilitate collection of information and later transcribed for analysis. Shortly after completion of the interviews, both participants received a copy of the transcript to give them an opportunity to confirm the accuracy of the conversation and to add or clarify any points in the transcription. Both participants were at ease and indicated no confusion about the questions or needed the questions reworded for clarification. Both participants appeared comfortable and relaxed in giving responses to the open-ended questions. Both the male and female pilot participants were open, confident with their responses, and elaborated on questions, which confirmed that the level of questions were clear and suitable for future volunteer participants. Based upon the pilot participants' clarity of understandability of the interview questions there were no changes to the interview questions. The participants were reassured participation in this study was voluntary. Participants received assurance that he or she were free to withdraw from this study at any time without any negative consequences by advising the researcher. The length of the interview lasted approximately 30 to 45 minutes including the preparation time reviewing the mutual consent form and obtaining signatures. Since there were no changes to the interview questions resulting from the pilot study, the two pilot study participants' responses became a part of the data collection for this study.

Findings

Following the pilot study, 10 more audio-recorded interviews took place. These 10 students began their first year of high school at the study's Central Texas school district mainstream high school and failed to earn credits to promote them with their freshman cohort class. The 10 participants, comprised of male and female volunteers, graduated from the credit-recovery nontraditional alternative high school in the Central Texas area. Immediately following each interview, transcription of the interviews occurred along with a face-to-face meeting with the participants to provide a written copy of the interview for their review. The participants then had the opportunity to member check by reviewing the transcription for accuracy of recording. All respondents agreed their transcriptions were accurate reflections of their responses.

Following the member checks, a co-rater assisted in identifying major themes present in the transcriptions. The co-rater and researcher coded the transcriptions independently. Both first coded all participants' responses to Interview Question 1, coded all responses to Interview Question 2, and continued using this same procedure for the 10 remaining interviews for all 12 participants. After both the co-rater and researcher coded all responses, a discussion of commonalities among their codes occurred. Three primary themes emerged and nine secondary themes developed. Figure 1 represents the three primary themes that emerged from the graduates responses.

A phenomenological, qualitative design was appropriate for this study because exploration of the perceptions of individuals occur (Creswell, 2012). The problem was that students were not earning sufficient credits to remain on grade level with their freshman level cohort and were at-risk of dropping out of school. The results of the study may identify processes that educators can use to coordinate programs for students who have experienced multiple failures in the mainstream high school. One central research question guided this study. RQ1: What are the graduates' perceptions of their credit-recovery nontraditional alternative high school and how did his or her experiences influence his or her graduation? The data consisted of 12

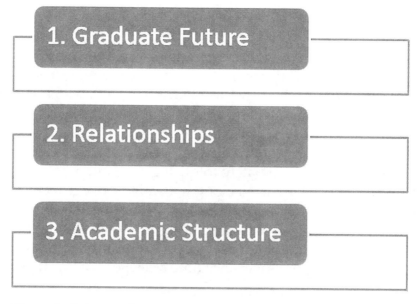

Figure 1. Primary themes.

face-to-face interviews; which included two interviews from the pilot study and the 10 interviews that followed the pilot study. All participants answered the same 10 interview questions. The interview questions' design was to allow the researcher to answer the central research question through a series of sub-questions. The five sub-questions embraced two interview questions each to support the central research question. These sub-questions (SQ) and interview questions (IQ) were:

SQ1.   What are the graduates' perceptions of their credit-recovery nontraditional alternative high school experience?

    IQ1.   Most students who attend credit-recovery nontraditional alternative high schools have multiple reasons for attending, what were yours?

    IQ6.   With your experiences in this credit-recovery nontraditional alternative high school, what would you suggest is needed to improve high school in general?

SQ2.   How did this experience help him or her achieve graduation?

    IQ2.   How did your experiences at this high school help you achieve graduation?

    IQ7.   When did you know, graduation from this high school was going to become a reality?

    SQ3.   How does the at-risk student's self-efficacy relate to the environment of their school?

    IQ3.   What were the influences that help you to graduate?

    IQ8.   Why did you take ownership in your learning at this credit-recovery nontraditional alternative high school?

SQ4.   What education practices foster increased achievement levels?

    IQ4.   Describe how the learning environment influenced your attendance?

    IQ9.   What are the outstanding features or characteristics of the faculty that encouraged you to graduate?

SQ5. What are the graduates' perceptions toward prevention of dropout rates?

> IQ5. What were your past high school experiences that hindered your success?

> IQ10. What educational practices kept you from dropping out of school?

Data analysis consisted of identifying thematic input from the participants' interviews and correlating participant input from the central research question of the study. Methodology and analysis used to identify the trends in the participant interviews related to the experiences of participants during their school experience while being a high school student. The interviews lasted approximately 30-45 minutes each. Every participant answered the same 10 questions.

The 12 graduate participants contributed his or her perceptions, experiences, expectations, and motivations about attending and graduating through a school, which allowed them to recover and accelerate high school course credit. Their responses generated three primary themes: (a) graduate future, (b) relationships, and (c) academic structure. Each of these primary themes had three secondary themes within each category.

Every participant offered many intriguing perspectives of their perception and examples of their experiences of attending a credit-recovery nontraditional alternative high school that they believed impactful for disenfranchised students' re-engagement to graduate high school. Since participant topics included various concerns of graduate future, relationships, and academic structure, these three emerged as the primary themes. Each of these primary themes had three secondary themes within its category. The next sections provide an in-depth analysis of the primary themes.

Primary Theme 1: Graduate Future

The perceptions and experiences of the graduates from the credit-recovery nontraditional alternative high school were overwhelmingly favorable towards the campus' practices and support of inspiring participant graduation. Every participant offered specific examples about the campus teachers, administrator, curriculum structure, and student development programs that influenced graduation. The secondary themes that emerged from this category included second chances, engagement, and graduation urgency. Figure 2 displays the secondary themes found within the primary theme of graduate future.

Secondary themes that evolved from Primary Theme 1, graduate future appeared in 100% of the participants' responses throughout the interviews. All participants stated his or her individual academic prowess, attendance, and behavior improved from their past mainstream performance. Eleven of the 12 participants believed graduation was in their future after entering into the credit-recovery nontraditional alternative high school. When the motivational speakers and mentors shared their experiences, it proved to be a positive influence on the participants. Participant G8 stated, "Like on career days when the people from the army came in and they told us stuff . . . it made you actually want to be something."

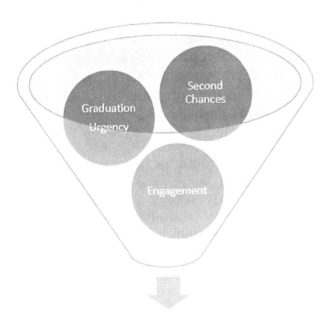

Graduate Future

Figure 2. Primary theme 1 and supporting secondary themes.

Secondary theme 1: Second chances. Each of the graduates acknowledged a sense of urgency for a second chance due to the possibility of their fate based on previous years of high school failures. The participants' realization was they did not earn high school credits at a pace to graduate with their cohort class, which led to no graduation or alternative credit-recovery program.

The first subtheme from the data related to 100% of participant responses addressing *second chances* by way of opportunities to participate in the campus special programs such as college tours, volunteer activities, speakers, and mentor visitation on the campus, which instilled an understanding and promise of a bright future after graduation. Specifically, second chances correlated with the opportunity to recover lost credits. Every participant addressed receiving a second chance to re-earn credits lost in early years in high school as the indicator that ignited the belief graduation was obtainable. "I think that answer would be, it just showed me that there is a second chance in life for all people" shared by Participant G2. For that reason, second chances emerged as Secondary Theme 1.

In particular, answers to the Interview Question SQ2-IQ7, "When did you know, graduation from this high school was going to become a reality?" Participant G1 stated, "When I just enjoyed coming. Like I didn't have a problem getting up going to school; when I looked forward to going to school." Participant G6 stated, "As soon as I got there. Yeah." Participant G8 stated,

> When I passed my TAKS test the first round and I had already completed my credits already. Cause I really didn't think I was gonna graduate prior to me coming over here; and when I see myself progressing and I see that studying for the TAKS test actually helped me. I knew I was gonna graduate.

Participant G12 stated,

> When I was down to like three credits . . . and just the easy credits, and then I had one speech to give to get out, and that's when I was pretty excited about it. I realized that I was about to be done, and I wasn't even afraid to get up in front of everybody and say what I had to say to get up. Spoke my mind, said what was off the top of my head, and I passed.

Secondary theme 2: Engagement. It was evident there were hindrances at their mainstream campus. Responding to SQ5-IQ5 and IQ10 participants talked about the hindrances as distractors to learning, attending school, and to promoting negative behavior. Three interview responses summed up the lack of engagement at the mainstream campus and re-engaging with the credit-recovery campus. Participant G1 stated,

> being in larger groups . . . I mean . . . I tend to act out more . . . the class wasn't at my pace so I tend to be a little ahead of the class and I'm sitting there bored, so I'm doing other things in class that I shouldn't be doing, or not to come to school.

Participant G5 stated,

> I wouldn't even want to blame it on the teachers. It was just pretty much me. Just being lazy and slacking on what I was doing. Um. . . and procrastinating. When you get a little bit older, you realize that you can't procrastinate because you'll never do it. So, that was one thing I learned in high school and I apply it today.

Participant G6 stated,

> I used to do all kinds of stuff over there. I think it would be getting in the wrong crowd. You know . . . I was in with . . . you know . . . what they're called gang bangers . . . you know . . . I don't know what it is now but being over there around that it just wasn't good for me. It got to the point where I was actually bringing . . . . to be honest with you I was bringing like spray paint cans to school. I went to each . . . probably still in my referrals . . . in fact it can even be pulled up . . . you know . . . just being around those kind of people didn't do good for me. Skipping school . . . driving off . . . walking off . . . not listening . . . walking . . . sleeping in class. You know . . . them teachers let it happen. You know it's not their fault though; it's my fault you know. I was just looking . . . I guess I was just looking for that extra push. That's all I needed.

Secondary theme 3: Urgency. Graduation Urgency emerged as a secondary theme during student responses to interview question SQ3-IQ8, "Why did you take ownership in your learning at this credit-recovery nontraditional alternative high school?" Ninety-nine percent of the participants stated the focus was to finish quickly so they could get on with their lives, start college, focus on their child, and/or work. Participant G1 stated,

> I wanted to be through with high school. I wanted to go ahead and get a jump-start on college. I was just tired of attending a regular school when I could come and complete my work at my own pace.

Participant G5 stated, "One reason is because I have a daughter. I had a daughter at the time. I think she was probably like three at the time. If I don't do it, who's going to do it." Participant G9 stated,

> the environment here is different than main stream high school. It was . . . its more quiet. It's more at your own pace. It helped me just to go at my own pace . . . um . . . go fast if I want to . . . .and other subjects if I needed to slow down or if I needed help I was able to get that.

The graduates expressed being behind became overbearing and the necessity to attend a school that existed for credit-recovery at an accelerated pace, echoed an urgency if they were to graduate. The state of urgency existed for these participants, and the following are quotes of how they felt about this situation. They said, "Pick up credits I lost, to graduate high school early due to young teen age pregnancy," "to graduate most of all, but when I was in school, it really didn't go well," "I was lacking two or three credits and I wasn't gonna be able to graduate, I was getting behind in high school," "Got off track and that was the best option for me," "My reasons were is because I was just not getting nothing done over there in the first three years. So I had to do something . . . last year . . . Senior. I had to make something," "To catch up on credits,"

> Well . . . I . . . at the time I had just had my son, so I was looking to go to a school that would help me graduate, and graduate at the year that I was supposed to have. I was behind,

"My reasons for attending? Um . . . it was due to the fact that I didn't have all the credits that I needed by the time . . . .and because of family problems also,"

I was a high school dropout. My mom's last wish was for me to get a high school diploma. So, I found an accelerated campus, therefore, I can get out on time, and not late, and fulfill my mom's wish.

With students being behind, knowing they were behind, and understanding the choices that could be corrected, recognized an earnestness of not settling for "I cannot or would not graduate," but the compulsion of getting to a place where additional support could be provided.

Primary Theme 2: Relationships

A student's decision to leave school affects a number of complex factors and is often the culmination of a long process of disengagement from school (Tyler & Lofstrom (2009). Students who struggle in school, especially those who disengaged, need both support and challenge to reconnect with learning and stay on a path to earn a high school diploma. Graduates shared their relationships with family, school staff, peers, and community members served as consistent monitors. Through the efforts of such a force students who were once deemed at-risk of dropping out found stability, motivation, and encouragement. It is apparent the relationships cultivated students' self-efficacy as it related to the environment of their school. The admiring influences of teachers and other staff members exposed students' self-efficacy endorsing a successful high school experience unveiling real options for the future.

Responses to SQ2 and SQ4 dealt with respondents' experiences at the alternative school that influenced their graduation through an environment, which fostered achievement and attendance. Additionally they were to share the characteristics of the faculty that encouraged achieving a goal of graduation. One-hundred percent of the respondents provided in-depth stories about the teachers and administration providing motivation and encouragement, self-paced learning, and computer-based instruction blended with one-on-one teacher instruction. Every participant had positive responses and examples of how the credit-recovery campus reached out to their needs and supported not only their academic success but also societal needs inside and outside of school.

Participants reported their attendance, behavior, and self-esteem improved. Participant responses included,

> I think for the most part it was more so all the teachers that en-couraged you. Like you have to do this because I guess when you sat down and talked to them, each person had their goal of exactly why they came to south campus and the teacher kept that in mind. Even if you decided you wanted to give up or quit, they kept saying "well remember you came here for this or that rea-son," the help from the principal and uh the teachers; and the students that I went back to school with were pretty cool.

Participants expressed their experiences with the curriculum as such, "it's self-paced so just being able to move faster and get things done quicker as opposed to having to sit there and listen to a lecture and do homework on their time it was better."

> The teachers . . . along with the principal . . . encouraging us and having speakers come to the school and . . . speakers that . . . had went through similar situations as us to motivate us and encour-age us and let us know that just because we're not going to a tra-ditional high school we can still graduate and make something of ourselves in the future.

Figure 3 displays Primary Theme 2 and the corresponding second-ary themes.

Themes regarding teacher and principal influence appeared in 97 responses throughout the 12 interviews. Graduates described their experiences with teachers in their mainstream high school teachers and compared those experiences to their credit-recovery nontradi-tional alternative high school teachers. Specifically, study participants referred to the lack of care and attention received from mainstream teachers and the attentiveness with care received from the teachers at the credit-recovery high school.

Secondary theme 4: Teacher and administration influence. Fifty-two positive responses indicated how the participants felt about their teach-ers at the alternative campus. There was no negative feedback about teachers in the credit-recovery nontraditional alternative high school. One participant referenced the administrator as "really good keeping

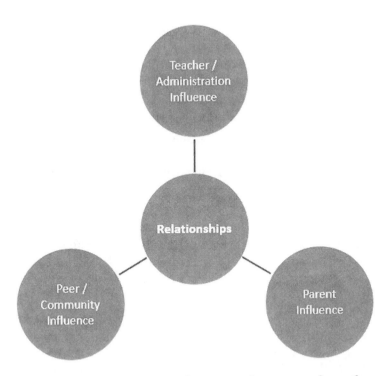

Figure 3. Primary theme 2 and supporting secondary themes.

everybody in line because we feared the principal definitely." Graduates recalled their experiences about their relationships and support from the teachers. The graduates acknowledged their teachers as caring adults who could help them overcome obstacles and find success despite the graduates' struggles. It was important to note the academic issue was not the only topic shared about their teachers. They revealed teachers' willingness to help plan their futures or even solve personal impasses. Graduates discussed the importance of the school staff being present for them and being an adult they could trust. The graduates talked about building positive relationships with teachers who helped them try harder academically and recognize they were not alone. When asked the interview question SQ4-IQ9, "What are the outstanding features or characteristics of the faculty that encouraged you to graduate?" Participant G1 stated

> They always encouraged you. They were friendly. They were willing to help you. It wasn't like they had a problem, or if they felt like

you were . . . trying to . . . they were willing to help you learn. They were willing to help you graduate; like they helped push you. If I didn't attend school they were like "why didn't you attend class?" "Why were you not here today"? Like they were . . . even if you didn't . . . if you needed a way to school, they were going to find a way for you to get there. Like they showed they cared.

Participant G2 stated,

Most of the teachers let a lot of things be hands on. We got to make comments and uh . . . we got to talk . . . we got to talk back to the teachers as well as the teachers got to talk to us, and they helped out as much as possible. Especially my science teacher. He was real cool. I liked him a lot. So, they were just real hands on, just let us express ourselves. I attended all the time . . . every day . . . every day. I wanted to be there too.

Participant G9 stated,

The teachers . . . along with the principal encouraging us and having speakers come to the school and . . . speakers that . . . had went through similar situations as us to motivate us and encourage us and let us know that just because we're not going to a traditional high school we can still graduate and make something of ourselves in the future.

Participant G10 stated,

The faculty . . . they're great. They . . . if I needed something, they're there to help me understand what I was learning about. Um . . . and just as they're the faculty but also, in a way, a friend because they understood what I was going through. I was trying to graduate, so they did what . . . the best they could to help me understand that.

Participant G11 stated, "Their personalities. Their personalities mostly, and uh the fact that they were honest about everything . . . constantly. It made me want to work harder." Participant G12 stated, "Teachers that stayed on my butt and kept me straight you know and kept me motivated to get my work done and get out . . . .the teachers."

Secondary theme 5: Parent influence. The second subtheme coded from the data related to the relationships and influence of graduates' parents. As shared in the literature review, high or low levels of student academic confidence, self-esteem, greater school engagement, fewer behavior problems, greater ambitions, and lower stress are contingent on emotional support from family structure (Christenson et al., 1992). Regardless of education level, ethnic background, or income level, parents want their kids to be successful in school; however, they do not know how to support their children (LaRocque et al., 2011). Family support is of major importance in predicting student achievement (Dornbusch & Ritter, 1988). Ten out of the 12 participants mentioned the influence of their parents and/or a family member.

In response to SQ3, "How does the at-risk student's self-efficacy relate to the environment of their school?" and IQ3, "What were the influences that helped you to graduate?" The graduates were adamant to prove to their parents he or she had the tenacity and commitment to earn a high school diploma. Several talked about how they had disappointed parent(s) in the past and were ready to make changes to make their parents happy and proud. Participant G1 stated,

> Influences of course, most of all, my mother who pushed me to graduate early. Um, second of all it was because being in a high school and trying to be a young mother, that was another influence that helped me graduate like a year early, along with . . . I mean . . . Everybody that was there was like "you can go ahead and you can do anything regardless of what the past that hindered you."

Participant G3 stated, "My parents and the teachers that pushed us. By making us work, focus on the work; try not to get off topic." Participant G4 stated, "My family helped me through it a lot, and the principal helped me through it also with her words of confidence." Participant G7 stated,

> Most likely my mom. It . . . .my mom is the one that kept pushing me too. When I didn't show up for school she would get after me. She would be like "well you need to go to school."

Participant G12, one of the two high school dropouts that returned to school at the credit-recovery campus had a deep conviction due to the influence of his mother. He shared repeatedly in question after question why he was committed to graduating this time around,

The fact that I wanted to make my mom proud, fulfill her last wish. My grandma supporting me when she didn't have to . . . taking me in when my mom passed away and wanting me to get a good education myself, so . . . I had pretty good motivations to get in and get out.

Secondary theme 6: Peer and community influence. The third subtheme coded from the data related to the influence of peers and community partners. Eight of 12 participants mentioned the positive effect of their peers. Responding to interview questions SQ4–IQ4 and IQ9, the participants shared experiences of self-monitoring behavior for themselves and others around them. They also talked about receiving encouragement and classroom help from peers. Many believed the challenge resulted when one of their peers graduated which became a motivating influence. In particular, Participant G7,

What kept me coming? Seeing friends that I thought you know . . . that you know . . . I thought they gave up and they were actually here the whole time. And they were worse than me. I thought to myself, well if they can do it then I can do it.

Participant G8 stated,

They were there for like help and support. Like motivation and . . . we all helped each other. Like if one of us had a question about something . . . . a subject that somebody else was stronger in . . . then we all were there to help each other.

Participant G9 stated,

Knowing that I was going to a school where I was surrounded by people that kind of knew my situation and understood what I was going through and were just very helpful . . . helpful and encouraging me to keep going to finish school and make something of myself, and just the environment that we had. I just felt comfortable.

Participants reported life changing and saving moments while engaged with community partnerships. This coded theme was worthy of mention due to the effect it had on the participants. The engagement of the community aided in the at-risk student achievement because more individuals invested in the success of the students. The participants reported they felt a connection with the community and the speakers that came to visit them on campus. Seven out of 12 participants reported the visits positively influenced their decision-making. Participants believed the community members genuinely cared about them and their future. Participant G7 stated,

> One single event. I wanna say when we had somebody attend over here. It was a guy and . . . you know . . . he like kinda rapped. And it was called Movement Up. You know . . . that dude kinda . . . you know . . . he was basically saying that you can be bad but you know you can all be changed. And so I was like . . . dude kinda inspired me a little bit. I still got the bracelet from that year too. I still have it all.

Participant G12 stated, "Going to Fort Hood, having to fill out college applications before we got out, all the cool stuff we got to actually do and all the cool people we got to meet during it . . . that was good experiences for me." Participant G9 stated,

> We had different groups . . . like on career days when the people from the army came in and they told us stuff . . . it made you actually want to be something. Not just come to school and if you graduate, you do and if you don't, you don't.

Participant G7 stated,

> I think it would have been like everything we used to do here from the experiments to even the field trips. Those inspired a lot of people you know. I have a friend that used to be in the same class. He's a marine now. And I remember him . . . that marine coming up to our school and talking to us. He said that inspired him too . . . so it's like you know . . . here . . . you know . . . they don't just give you one thing to do you know. Multiple things . . . to people coming over here . . . motivational speakers . . . to experiments you know . . . one on one . . . just not a piece of paper in here. If I could come back again I would. That's all I know. I love this school. I really do. I didn't want to leave.

Participant G11 stated,

> I don't think there was anything negative about the school that I came upon at all. Just like Fort Hood for instance or the mentors that would come in. They were just encouraging. Like really

encouraging. And then they told us about their . . . gave us their testimony and made us want to work harder basically.

Primary Theme 3: Academic Structure

Graduates interviewed gave various examples of instructional approaches supporting the academic structure of the credit-recovery nontraditional alternative high school. This study revealed 100% of the study participants attended the credit-recovery nontraditional alternative high school because they were behind academically and were high-risk for dropping out of school prior to attending the credit-recovery nontraditional alternative high school. Two of the participants had already dropped out.

Earning high school course credit is the main factor for high school graduation. Some students fail to graduate because they are unsuccessful in earning the credits needed to graduate (Allensworth & Easton, 2005, p. 1). Watson and Gemin (2008) shared the credit-recovery short-term goal was to help freshmen recover course credits forfeited due to failure. The long-term goals were to reduce the dropout rate and ultimately contribute to a high graduation rate for freshmen cohort classes. Researchers revealed credit-recovery programs allowed students to recover credits, and fostered the opportunity for students to stay on track for graduation with their freshman cohort (Pemberton, 2011; Trotter, 2008; Watson & Gemin, 2008).

Rumsberger (2001) introduced two programmatic approaches to students dropping out due to academic failure and/or behavior issues.

> One approach is to provide supplemental services to students within an existing school program. The second approach is to provide an alternative school program either within an existing school (school within a school) or in a separate facility (alternative school). Both approaches do not attempt to change existing institutions serving most students, but rather create alternative programs or institutions to target students who are somehow identified as at-risk of dropping out. (p. 26)

The secondary themes that emerged from the academic support category included learning style, size, pace, and speed. Figure 4 displays the third primary theme and the corresponding secondary themes.

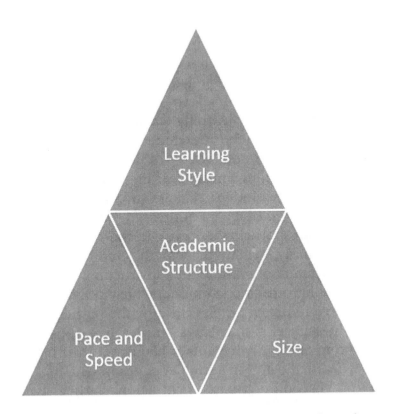

Figure 4. Primary theme 3 and supportive secondary themes.

Themes regarding academic structure received comments from 100% of the participants. Interview questions SQ1-IQ1 and IQ6 garnered the most responses about the academic structure of the credit-recovery nontraditional alternative high school. This theme appeared in 86 answers throughout the interviews with all 12 participants. One student said, "There is positive where I had tutoring in the summer and that helped me get my credits as well." Participants spoke about tutorials, tutoring, computer-based instruction, one-on-one help from teachers, hands-on, book study, self-paced projects, focus on work, on topic/off topic, doing paperwork, the learning environment, and group learning. These responses revealed approaches in the academic structure as being the theme and subthemes.

Secondary theme 7: Learning styles. Learning style was a major component of meeting the needs of at-risk students who have demonstrated multiple academic failures. Since not all students learn in the same way, curriculum and instruction design must be resourceful and inventive to meet the needs of students who are behind. Teachers' pedagogical skills must demonstrate ability to prepare and adjust teaching strategies for struggling learners as well as for those who seek acceleration. Differentiating learning was a major component of meeting the needs of students who attended the credit-recovery nontraditional alternative high school. Since skill levels vary from student to student, teachers must know about learning differences and do what they can to help every student achieve success. Study participants talked about how their teachers addressed learning based on their perspectives. Study participants revealed the academic structure as meeting their learning style by the way the credit-recovery programs offered via computer software, online instruction, or teacher-guided instruction (small group or one-on-one) which targeted the standards in which they were deficient. Specifically, the participants indicated tutoring for the state assessments was important to their success. One hundred percent of the participants talked about their learning styles, sharing they learned better in a smaller environment, in self-paced instruction, and via computer-based instruction. Participant G1 stated,

> I mean if you have the opportunity to work on your own and attend self-paced. I've always never really been a traditional student. I've always more so wanted to do accelerated courses. So for me it was beneficial for me because I'm not in a classroom where I have to wait. I'm able to work at my own pace instead of the teachers directing the learning experience. It helped me graduate because I was able to recover credits that I lost or a class that I had failed or something. I was able to pick it up back into my curriculum instead of attending summer school. That way as long as you're doing that you're able to, obviously you're able to gain more credits and you can probably graduate with a higher diploma than what you would have graduated with.

Participant G8 stated,

> It . . . especially the system, it let you go through a lesson but it let you test out of it if you didn't need it so it didn't slow you down. And it showed you what you needed help with and you ask for help and the teachers are here to study with you and help you

study. They made sure that you knew what you needed to know, or that's how I felt when I passed my test. I guess it's smaller over here so they have more time and you can stay after school and most of these teachers are coaches . . . and it was just a better learning environment over here, but I think I got behind because I wasn't . . . having a problem paying attention in class and I couldn't get the extra help and tutoring that I needed.

Participant G9 stated,

Math wasn't my best subject so I got to go at a slower pace than that and then work my way up and get the tutoring that I needed, and that helped me a lot being able to move at my own pace.

Secondary theme 8: Size. The size of the school and class was significant to the participants. One hundred percent of the study participants talked about not fitting well in the mainstream high school structure or classes due to the size of the student population. When asked the question SQ1-IQ6, with your experiences in this credit recovery nontraditional alternative high school, "What would you suggest is needed to improve high school in general?" Eight of twelve participants referred to size. Participant G1 stated,

High school in general I feel like the classes are too large. Some students cannot . . . are not able to interact in a large setting because they're worried about what other students may think or they're thinking about what other students will say if they're . . . um . . . if they're holding the other class back because some other students in the class may be way . . . a little bit more intelligent than others and they're ready to move on verses somebody who's struggling in that subject.

Participant G5 stated, "Kind of being thrown into what feels like an ocean of people and we're all different but we're being all treated kind of the same and um . . . it just wasn't enough."

Seven of the 12 study participants referred positively to the size in terms of class size of the credit-recovery nontraditional alternative high school. Responses included,

I was in a smaller group setting where I was able to get more help from a teacher. It was a lot more relaxed than it was at mainstream campus, so it was a better seem like I got more attention. It wasn't as many students to a teacher and we had more programs. There was more motivation over here and more programs to help us study for the TAKS test. The environment was real good. It was uh . . . it was real even toned. I liked it. I liked the experience a lot. The learning environment was a smaller setting. I had more one on one time with the teacher.

Secondary theme 9: Pace and speed. One hundred percent of the study participants referenced the environment throughout the interviews. "It's self-paced so just being able to move faster and get things done quicker as opposed to having to sit there and listen to a lecture and do homework on their time it was better," echoed one participant. Repeatedly, all 12 participants linked the pace and speed to the environment as a factor that supported an expeditious graduation. Opportunity to work at your own pace and speed emerged as a secondary theme. Participants talked about the environment being calm, safe, and relaxed. What revealed the pace and speed of the environment produced a motivation to be present at school each day. One participant stated,

> My attendance . . . I don't think I missed any . . . no. I just wanted to get everything done. It makes me want to get things done faster when you realize like how much easier it is basically, I mean it was self-paced, so I was able to move at my own pace instead of with the class.

Other participants shared,

> I was just looking to go to a school that would help me accomplish getting graduated in the year that I was supposed to. I had to hurry up and graduate so I could get a job and start working making money.

> "Yeah . . . yeah. Just the fact that I could get in, get my work done and get out and graduate on time instead of two years . . . three years late was pretty awesome." Participants in this study believed attending the credit-recovery nontraditional alternative high school personally connected their learning and themselves to the real world. Many of the participants discussed how behind they were in terms of graduation and how they pursued diligently

to attend the school. The graduates believed the credit-recovery high school connected them to the right teachers, instruction, programs, motivation, and engagement that increased the reality of them becoming a high school graduate.

Summary

Chapter 4 included three primary themes discovered through the study of perceptions and experiences of graduates from credit-recovery nontraditional alternative high schools. The four-pronged approach first explored credit-recovery students' experiences with their credit-recovery nontraditional alternative high school. The second approach was to focus on Hoyle's (1998) problematic, yet valid, concern that students feel powerless in the school environment. The third determined if alternative education practices foster increased achievement levels, and lastly exposed those areas preventing at-risk students from being successful in high school. The three primary themes were graduate future, relationships, and academic structure. Within those three primary themes, nine secondary themes emerged: (a) second chances, (b) engagement, (c) graduation urgency, (d) teacher/administration influence, (e) parent/family influence, (f) peer/community influence, (g) learning styles, (h) size, and (i) speed and pace.

There were no outliers. All 12 participants had affirmative perceptions and experiences toward the credit-recovery nontraditional alternative high school. All participants noted that in order to be successful once they had fallen behind one must want it for themselves. When asked, what they suggested to improve high schools in general, the responses were specific:

> Not labeling everybody as what you think they are, not looking at everyone as a statistic, actually try to get to know the students as opposed to "oh he's wearing baggy pants and a long t-shirt, he's probably stupid. Let's throw him in remedial."

One graduate responded with, "I feel like if they would stop having these pre-set ideas about people then they would be able to be more successful if they make students feel like they actually care about them." Several suggested, coming up with ways to encourage the kids to keep going including pushing them to go to school, coming up with new ways to keep them involved, and keeping them wanting to come to school, and more one-on-one with students and teachers because that is probably the key to a student succeeding. In conclusion, Participant G12 was very specific and talked about applying his high school experience to his current occupation. He stated,

> Group learning . . . I think. Actually what we're doing at my job right now is uh . . . trying new things . . . making different kinds of desks where more than one person can sit a desk at a time so you're not just learning by yourself and a teacher standing up front talking. It's a group-learning thing and that's what my job is. I work at Artco Bell. We make school furniture. So, we're trying to experiment with new things for new different types of learning.

Using the above-mentioned themes, Chapter 5 consists of recommendations and implications. The first section includes a summary of the study, then recommendations, and finally future research. Chapter 5 is the conclusion of the study.

CHAPTER 5

Recommendations And Implications

The purpose of this qualitative phenomenological research study was to explore the graduates' perceptions of credit-recovery nontraditional alternative high schools. The focus of this study had a four-pronged approach, which included an exploration of credit-recovery graduates' experiences with their credit-recovery nontraditional alternative high school, to determine if students feel powerless in the school environment, to determine if alternative education practices increased achievement levels, and finally to determine those areas preventing at-risk students from being successful (Lagana-Riordan et al., 2011).

The study involved interviewing 12 participants, two participants from the pilot study and 10 participants from the purposeful sampling of the first 12, who responded to the invitation to participate in this study. High school graduates who attended and graduated from a credit-recovery nontraditional alternative high school exploring their perceptions and experiences. This was a diversified group by age and other demographics representing five graduating classes. By examining the reasons for multiple failures in mainstream high school and experiences in a credit-recovery nontraditional alternative school, school districts, administrators, and policymakers may identify potential solutions that may result in effective practices for re-engaging disenfranchised students.

Summary of the Study

When students fail courses, fail to achieve promotion, or drop out of school, the result is detrimental to the student and to the school district (Dessoff, 2009). The general problem is perennially, significant percentages of high school students do not graduate because they are behind in grade-level credits (Allensworth & Easton, 2005; Kennelly & Monrad, 2007; Rumberger, 2001). The average high school student earns an estimated 6.5 credits per year for promotion to the next grade level (Texas Education Agency, 2013). When this does not occur, students require nontraditional options to motivate them to obtain the necessary credits for graduation in four years.

The findings of recent studies validate the results of this study regarding alternative schools operated by the school district typically provide structure, coursework, and class time to better accommodate the work schedules and parenting responsibilities of students who have left or are contemplating leaving school (Tyler & Lofstrom, 2009). The finding of Streeter et al. (2011) validated students who attended an academic nontraditional alternative school for at-risk youth earned more credits and have higher graduation rates than their peers who continued to attend traditional schools.

Over the years, many graduation support programs became high schools. The focus of these high schools is on dropout prevention programs as an intervention and means to providing students with the support needed to stay in school. Many transformations of alternative education have taken place throughout the years leading to various forms of graduation support.

> Students needing to make up credit toward graduation, often called credit recovery has one or more of the characteristics of students considered to be at-risk for failing to eventually graduate from high school. Opportunities for students who struggle to catch up on credit can make a difference between graduation and dropping out of school. (Shore & Shore, 2009, as cited in Pemberten 2011, p. 2)

Documentation within the literature review focused primarily on historical facts of characteristics of nontraditional alternative schools, at-risk students, and credit-recovery programs. The literature evidenced relevant reviews of a broad base to support credit-recovery options in nontraditional and alternative schools. The problem merits attention since every year more than a million children leave school without a traditional high school diploma (Dessoff, 2009; Heckman & LaFontaine, 2010; Keller, 2014; Tyler & Lofstrom, 2009). The lived experiences explored in this study may help school leaders, teachers, staff, parents, and community partners understand the unique needs of this population.

Thirty students who attended and graduated from the credit-recovery nontraditional alternative high school received an invitation to participate in the study. The first 12 responding with a yes who met the criteria were the participants. All respondents participated in a 30-45 minute audio-recorded interview. All interviews were one-on-one. The interviews consisted of 10 questions. The responses to these questions provided the data to answer the research question: "What are the graduates' perceptions of their credit-recovery nontraditional alternative high school and how did his or her experiences influence his or her graduation?" Five sub-questions supported the central research question:

1. What are the graduates' perceptions of their credit-recovery nontraditional alternative high school experience?

2. How did this experience help him or her achieve graduation?

3. How does the at-risk student's self-efficacy relate to the environment of their school?

4. What education practices foster increase achievement levels?

5. What are the graduates' perceptions toward prevention of dropout rates?

Before beginning this research project, a review of literature, resulted in 116 references. The review of literature represented three sections covering 17 topics related to the study of the research question. The historical overview covered three areas. The first was high school dropout statistics, identifying the characteristics which identify students who are at-risk to drop out. Texas Education Agency Public Education Information Management System (PEIMS) TEC

§29.081, Compensatory and Accelerated Instruction (2012-2013) reports 13 characteristics of a student at risk of dropping out of school. All participants in the study met one or more of the drop out characteristics. The second was Student and Family Characteristics related to the role of family support affecting education. One hundred percent of participants in the study talked about the support and positive influence of family and community. Each participant told about how family encouraged him or her to stay in school to earn a high school diploma. This section included a conflicting finding: "Among the strongest family domain dropout predictors are parental education, occupation, and income-in other words socioeconomic status" (Tyler & Lofstrom, 2009, p. 85). Raywid (1989) reported family background, socioeconomic status, and environment influences whether a student will succeed in school but LaRocque et al. (2011) found students with proper goal setting, educational techniques, encouragement, and support from school and community can exhibit resilience and grow to relish new challenges. The results of this study correlate more with LaRocque et al. (2011). The third section offered Maslow's hierarchy of needs, establishing hierarchy humanistic orientation to learning is evident within the social and environmental confines (McLeod, 2007). Humanistic needs comprised of physiological, safety, love, and self-esteem are needs of survival. Rising to level five, self-actualization is the peak of the hierarchy of motivation and desire for self-fulfillment.

In the next section, Theoretical Framework, the researcher examined student behaviors, perceptions, intrinsic and extrinsic motivation, population characteristics, past and current attitudes, beliefs, opinions, and practices (Creswell, 2008). The theoretical framework helped the researcher form the interview questions. By examining topics like scaffolding theory, self-determination theory, and Bandura's self-efficacy theory using the interview questions to garner responses provided better understanding about the graduates' perceptions of their credit-recovery nontraditional alternative high school. The data provided from participant responses, reinforced Vygotsky's zone of proximal development, which describes a student's next stage in learning (Yuanying, 2011). The next stage was the opportunity to participate in a credit-recovery program, which allowed students to work individually on work they were capable of completing. Gregory, Pugh, and Smith (1981) found that "alternative students reported much greater satisfaction with their schooling experiences than did students in traditional schools" (as cited in De La Ossa, 2005, p. 26). Students, who participate in credit-recovery programs, earn credits, and successfully complete state assessments, accepted learning as a process.

As mentioned earlier, the final section of the literature review entitled Current Findings comprised of 11 topics. These topics provided relevance based on Bullock (2007), the rapid growth of nontraditional alternative education programs in the 21st century was empowered by the mismatch between traditional schools' expectations and students' performance and/or behavior. Rix and Twining (2007) reported meeting the full range of needs presented by learners is the goal of current nontraditional alternative educational programs. Alternative education embraced success by providing a safe and caring haven for youth. The responsibility for providing free and appropriate education for all children is the law.

The final four topics (Cultural Relevant Leadership, Credit-Recovery Programs, Variations in Credit-Recovery Program Types, and Characteristics of Effective Credit-Recovery Programs) focused on the pedagogical techniques and identified trends related to the experiences and perceptions of curriculum, instruction, and the environment of the high school. The participants mentioned various instructional strategies including hands-on techniques, technology via computer-based curriculum and instruction, and multiple perspective learning. The strategies known as effective and engaging techniques are the best practices in credit-recovery nontraditional alternative high schools. Results revealed credit-recovery programs allowed students to recover credits, and fostered the opportunity for students to stay on track for graduation with their freshman cohort (Pemberton, 2011; Trotter, 2008; Watson & Gemin, 2008).

Many successful models of alternative education in the form of charter schools, private schools, and public alternative education centers may exist under the umbrella of school districts. These schools not only teach curriculum and practice pedagogy, but also provide guidance related to the social woes surrounding students, parents, and society (Sagor, 1999). Based on the themes that emerged from the data indicated the findings of this study could advance the means by which students engaged in useful learning remain in school earning enough credits to graduate. If the experiences at credit-recovery nontraditional alternative high schools increase the graduation rate of at-risk students, then identifying those experiences may help others toward a pathway to graduation. In many school districts, the traditional high school experience is simply counterproductive for some students.

Knowledge gained from this study may identify processes that educators can use to coordinate programs for students who have experienced multiple failures in the mainstream high school. Participants lived experiences explored in this study may help school leaders, teachers, staff, parents, and community partners understand the unique needs of this population. Finally, schools looking to establish a credit-recovery system may have better insight concerning pedagogy, curriculum, and students' socio-emotional needs.

Recommendations

In progressive education, the main purpose of instruction and discipline is to prepare students to be successful citizens in a democratic society by adjusting instruction to incorporate the experiences of students (Dewey, 1938). Participants in the current study shared their urgency to find a path to graduation and a traditional high school diploma. Through the process, participants owned their past transgressions and made sacrifices to improve. Wright (2012) reported there is an urgency for a new public education system design and implementation which demands inclusiveness to meet the needs of this century while meeting today's criteria of success for all students. The results of this study indicate how credit-recovery provides a resolution and is in the forefront of restructuring public education. The new public education system requires a design and implementation to meet the needs of this century and gain buy-in from the federal and state government, the community at-large, and school administrators. The results of the study indicate there is an urgent need for school choice by way of nontraditional educational options (Wolk, 2010).

Student characteristics associated with a greater possibility of not earning high school course credit, often termed the at-risk population, are at a greater chance of not graduating high school than other students. Poor school performance, low-test scores, course failures, and grade retention have all been found to strongly associate with leaving school before earning a high school diploma (Tyler & Lofstrom, 2009). Weak student engagement in the mainstream schools, often measured by absenteeism and discipline problems is also associated with disenfranchised students. Students inundated with early adult responsibilities, such as out of work greatly affect educational outcomes, and are commonly viewed as important predictors of schooling achievement.

Three primary themes emerged from the data: (a) graduate future, (b) relationships, and (c) academic structure. These themes support re-engagement of disenfranchised students who have experienced multiple academic failures. The themes also show how the role of societal failures require the involvement of the entire community not just the schools. The entire community must prioritize the needs of these at-risk populations in every aspect of education, from how to identify failing students earlier through assessment to determining appropriate resources for sustainable alternative systems.

Within graduate future, three secondary themes emerged. The first secondary theme was second chances. The next theme was engagement. The final secondary theme was graduation urgency. The results of the study confirmed failing courses in the ninth grade is a powerful predictor of dropping out. Participants talked about the opportunity for a second chance, how engagement in credit-recovery curriculum and instruction as well as the alternative school programming complimented their learning style, and the urgent need to fast track credit completion for graduation.

Due to the overwhelming state of lost course credits, a challenge exists for educators toward changing traditional practices to affect educational transformation for students who have become disengaged and disenfranchised. Rumberger (2011) reported the finding in a national study,

> On time graduates earned an average of almost 26 credits over their four years of high school, or about 6.6 credits per year.

> Students who dropped out of tenth grade had earned only 3.9 credits in their freshman year, which means they were most likely behind in their credits. Similarly, students who dropped out in the eleventh grade had earned 4.4 credits by the end of the tenth grade. This means that if that state or district required more than 17 credits to graduate they too, were behind in credits by the end of their sophomore year. Overall the results of the national study show that the fewer credits students earn in high school, the earlier they are likely to dropout. (p. 29)

Not one participant in this study wanted to remain a dropout.

The first recommendation presented is the establishment and a restructuring of an early identification process for identifying students in need of credit-recovery and/or nontraditional alternative learning opportunity. School districts should develop an alternative option or enhance already structured specialized instructional and personal development programs and plans for disenfranchised students who are in danger of dropping out or have already dropped out. This alternative option by way of an accredited credit-recovery nontraditional alternative high school campus should serve as a Response to Intervention (RTI) for eligible students who are (a) behind in credits and require credit-recovery and/or acceleration to earn graduate status, (b) has experienced personal, family, or other issues which have hindered academic success and/or attendance in the traditional school setting, (c) has demonstrated frustration with school and expresses a desire for positive change, (d) has a job or adult responsibilities (e.g., teen parent) that require a flexible schedule, and (e) any student who may require an alternate setting for learning smaller environment (Rumberger 2011). This structure should consist of a student identification process, enrollment process, attendance and discipline plan and procedures, curriculum and instruction implementation, specialized programming (i.e., guidance counseling and community involvement), and staff development.

The next recommendation is for mainstream high school administration to conduct frequent credit verification checkpoints to monitor students' progress and identify those who have failed courses and are behind. A recommendation is administrators create an identification process based on a RTI model. In addition, students identified as earning less than 5 credits their freshman year and students in higher grade levels who are 3.5 credits behind should be targeted for these alternative options. Identify these students before they become 17 years old and set up a system for recommendation. District administrators should develop an application process for student requests for enrollment if not an open enrollment option. District administration should accommodate school/program capacity/enrollment opportunities to eliminate student waiting lists.

Student achievement increases when the core capacity to meet the diverse needs of individual students' targets to attract and retain highly qualified teachers and support staff who are willing to practice culturally relevant pedagogy. The structure recommended to address relationships should have a staff of nurturing diverse certified teachers and highly accessible administrators reflective of the student population group they teach. Educational aides, Nurse, SRO, Diagnosticians, Truancy Officers, teen parenting program, post-secondary and financial aid planning, and mentoring programs should exist to meet the needs of these diverse student.

Another recommendation relevant for student engagement is for staff to teach beyond the classroom by utilizing outside resources (people, places, and things) to develop meaningful activities. Develop learning labs that include field trips to colleges, military bases, business tours, museums, marinas, and parks to name a few. Load up buses with students, microscopes and other scientific field testing instruments, and conduct live collaborative learning labs. Provide staff with budgets to purchase manipulatives that provide students with opportunities to explore by sight, touch, and taste that fosters curiosity for active exploration. Allow students to highlight their talents, which empower them to shape the school into a place they love to be and respect (Dewey, 1938).

Based on the analysis of data and overall participants' responses emerged Primary Theme 2; relationships and subthemes, where teachers, administrators, parents, and community influence play a vital role. These influences may enable many at-risk students to complete their high school diploma, prepare for college, and become quality workers and productive citizens. Successful programming begins with relationships. Undoubtedly, teachers' influence is the common denominator and ultimate factor of influence toward student and school success. With teachers being the most significant influence, the next recommendation is for teachers to establish and/or continue committed personal and private learning communities (PLCs) which involve common planning periods with content or grade level colleagues. Teacher involvement in important school decisions, flexibility, and understanding is indicative to influencing a student's mental life. Create supportive teaching and learning environments for all learners, where teachers and students feel confident in trying new things, being creative, and being critical in their thinking and application for learning.

Research has indicated student learning improves and academic goals are met when school staff has access to effective professional development (Fullan, 2001; Zepeda, 2004). A comprehensive plan for professional development should be based on a shared vision developed in a collaborative process by the education partners involved. The campus level professional development planning process should begin with an overview of the nontraditional alternative school's mission to serve, ongoing reviews of campus and student data, review of literature to support program implementation strategies, discussions to ensure alignment of content area curriculum with the district high school and the role of various education partners. Taking the time to develop the shared vision for professional development helps meet the needs of all parties and address unique contextual issues of the nontraditional learning environment, the classroom, and district goals. This collaborative approach fosters commitment to each other, the students, and families served which influences community behavior, teacher moral, pupil learning, and parent involvement.

Students along with their parent or guardian should have a required initial visit with the campus administrator, campus counselor, and teacher to review their personal data, personalized academic and social development plan. An informed community fosters a personal stake in learning, therefore sharing data with students and parents to maintain environments that cultivate knowledge, innovation, and participation. Overall, culture and climate should be in a constant state of inventiveness, excellence, and high expectations that has engaged partnerships with parents, businesses, and the community. Participants in the study shared support from campus speakers who talked about their jobs and careers that inspired them to feel connected to local business and community.

Within Primary Theme 3, Academic Structure, and subthemes learning style, size, pace, and speed were significant. Participants reported their achievement strengths were established through the opportunity to work at their own pace using online computer-based curriculum and instruction supplemented with offline projects and assignments. The overall goal should be to improve student performance, stimulate an aspiration to catch up on credits, and ultimately an expedited route to graduate. Differentiated instruction should improve by high margins student attendance and behavior patterns and performance on state and national assessments. Another recommendation is for small-size classes (1:15 ratio) with traditional instruction and nontraditional credit earning options.

A recommendation is for educators to focus on a process to involve academic assessments, both formative and summative, to assess teaching and learning, and to modify instruction based on student performance. A hybrid learning model comprised of on-line computer-based curriculum, direct teach component, collaborative, and group project-based learning model is suggested. Throughout the school year data should be analyzed and adjustments made to improve instruction through means of the RTI process. Small group pullout and double blocked core classes should provide intense remediation and tutorials to all students, struggling learners, and those who were severely behind.

Additionally, RTI is to make data relevant with all involved individuals. This will institutionalize a meaningful and useful setting for academic learning, individualize learning, and provide an instructional focus on social behavioral development, which incorporates responsibility and leadership. Family, community members, and parent opportunity for involvement at a credit-recovery nontraditional alternative high school should be an organized, ongoing review for improvement that includes a school-wide plan for the development of the parent involvement policy and parent compact. Parents, families, and community members have opportunities to participate in the campus site-based decision making (SBDM) and district education improvement committees (DEIC). SBDM and DEIC are comprised of community, parent, and district staff representatives who assist, guide, and make recommendations to school district improvement plans as well as board policy. Parent communication with by way of various sources, which include district and campus orientation, parent participation should be a requirement for enrollment, student portfolios, utilization of administrative office and counseling department to make community contacts and develop meaningful programs, nine-week progress reports, parent surveys, teacher/parent weekly communication - 3 positives comments to 1 negative ratio, and include parents as mentors and volunteers on campus, to name a few.

Indisputably, this at-risk population needs additional academic and social supports. Many national education systems, such as the Dutch and Finland educational systems tend to channel students into particular pathways at an early age, with a few opportunities to redirect course direction (Ripley 2013). In contrast, school systems and districts across the United States system lean towards offering second-chance options that can allow for redirections These second chance options allows U.S. school systems alternative opportunity to re-engage disenfranchised students by way of credit-recovery nontraditional alternative high schools (Tyler & Lofstrom, 2009). This study targeted graduates' perspectives and experiences, labeled by several participants as second-chance options. The credit-recovery nontraditional alternative schools serve as a school of choice; the second-chance option for the study participants, who made the decision to reconnect with school, was to attempt graduating with a traditional high school diploma and pursue a marketable skill.

The final recommendation is Dewey's (1938) progressive education. In progressive education, the main purpose of instruction and discipline is to prepare students to be successful citizens in a democratic society by adjusting instruction to incorporate the experiences of students (Dewey, 1938). Dewey's educational philosophy helped advance the *progressive education* movement, and introduced the development of *experiential education* programs and experiments. Dewey believed that students should be involved in real-life tasks and challenges in learning the content fields. An example is teaching math through learning proportions in cooking and history through how people lived. Dewey (1938) stated,

> "It is not too much to say that an educational philosophy which profess to be based on the idea of freedom may become as dogmatic as ever was the traditional education which is reacted against. For any theory or set of practices is dogmatic which is not based upon critical examination of its own underlying principles. Let us say that the new education emphasizes the freedom of the learner. (p. 22)

Connecting education as the economic power that is in a globalized technology world of knowledge, more experiential opportunities could advance second chances for students who need hands-on experiences to stay engaged in school. "The intensified participation of economic interests in education is not accidental" (Dewey, 1938, p. 39). Economic globalization requires the creation of a skilled labor force and the connection between education and economic productivity has increased pressures on the educational systems. Educational entrepreneurs see schools as the new business arena (Brown & Tannock, 2009; Stromquist, 2002).

This final recommendation involves a progressive innovation establishment of credit-recovery nontraditional alternative high school partnerships with businesses by co-locating. The partnerships should strategically center curriculum and pedagogy on a specific career path and soft skills curriculum that would advance the marketability of these students and schools. These schools should be encouraged in industries such as retail, manufacturing, transportation ports, technology hubs, financial institutions, hospitals, and post-secondary institutions.

Future Research

The purpose of this qualitative phenomenological research study was to explore the graduates' perceptions of credit-recovery nontraditional alternative high schools. The investigator relied on 12 interviews with graduates of a credit-recovery nontraditional alternative high school. Since the data came from graduate perspectives, future researchers may interview enrolled students on strategies they believe contribute to effective processes at a credit-recovery nontraditional alternative high school. Additionally, while this study focused on graduates, an additional study may focus on students who attended a credit-recovery nontraditional alternative high school but were not successful. This may provide additional insight about the productivity of these schools.

Since 100% of the participants talked about their credit-recovery nontraditional alternative high school teachers, future research may include a focus on characteristics of teachers, administrators, and other staff who teach at credit-recovery nontraditional alternative high schools. This may provide a deeper understanding of both teaching strategies and overall pedagogical practices. Instead of relying on teacher perspectives, future research may investigate the correlation of specific strategies to student achievement or lack thereof. A study of the effects of individual environments with the alternative school is another area to explore. This research could help school leaders understand how to help teachers in general create best practices while working with this unique population.

Summary and Conclusions

The rising movement of nontraditional alternative schools has significant value on breaking the cycle of inequality and inequity. Kim and Taylor (2008) cited many reasons for the movement such as school accountability pressures, preventing student dropout, and creating environments for specialized academic rigor and successes. To satisfy the need for choice and diversity (Conley, 2002), the popularity of alternative education regained its momentum in the mid-1990s in the form of public and private voucher programs, charter schools, and magnet programs. In this study, there was a focused effort to obtain students' perspectives to discover ways to provide better educational opportunities for disenfranchised and/or disengaged students.

To promote positive development for disenfranchised or disengaged students and expand goals for school and beyond, educators must inspire students to acquire not only knowledge but also social understanding through useful activity like solving real problems or social challenges. The findings of this study clearly indicate an opportunity to achieve meaningful change through redesigning schools to meet the needs of individual students. "To appreciate the power of personalizing education, one has to spend time with the students – listen to their stories, engage them in conversation, and see how motivated and confident they are" (Wolk, 2010, p. 21).

This qualitative phenomenological research study was an exploration of lived experiences from 12 graduates of a credit-recovery nontraditional alternative high school. Research by Wolk (2010), Tyler and Lofstrom, (2009), Rumberger, (2011), and Dewey, (1938) authenticated the findings of this study based on the participants' responses to the research questions and the sub-questions about their perceptions and experiences in their credit-recovery nontraditional alternative high school.

In conclusion, knowledge gained from this study may identify processes that educators can use to coordinate programs for students who have experienced multiple failures in the mainstream high school. The lived experiences explored in this study may help school leaders, teachers, staff, parents, and community partners understand the unique needs of this population. Finally, schools looking to establish a credit-recovery system may have better insight concerning pedagogy, curriculum, and students' socio-emotional needs.

"While a large array of individual attitudes, behaviors, and aspects of individual educational performance influence dropping out and graduation these individual factors shaped by institutional settings are where children live" (Rumberger, 2011, p. 7). Alternative schools are not a dumping ground to get rid of kids who were disruptions on mainstream campuses. It is a phenomenon of high numbers of students from the mainstream high schools who are not on track to graduate with their cohort class. There is an urgent need to focus efforts toward creating schools that nurture the desire of students who need another chance to do better. "You cannot measure what counts in education – the human qualities" (Ripley, 2013, p. 13).

Each year an average of 1.2 million students drop out of school, tantamount to one student every 26 seconds (Dessoff, 2009). Rumberger

(2011) reported that Education Weekly estimates 1.3 million students in 2010 failed to graduate. This means the nation's schools are losing more than 7,000 students each day (Rumberger 2011). One student every 26 seconds dropping out of school is a detriment to the future economic growth of the United States (Dessoff, 2009). The findings of this study could advance the means by which students engaged in useful learning to remain in school earning enough credits to graduate. If the experiences at credit-recovery nontraditional alternative high schools increase the graduation rate of at-risk students, then identifying those experiences may help others toward a pathway to graduation. This is a calling for support from across the district, local businesses, civic leaders, elected officials, philanthropists, the religious community, and regional social organizations. With a committed collaboration, an educational eco-system develops that supports multiple deliveries of education to meet the need of students.

References

Afterschool Alert. (2009, August). *Afterschool: Providing a successful route to credit attainment and recovery* (Issue Brief No. 39). Washington, DC: Nellie Mae Educational Foundation.

Allensworth, E. M., & Easton, J. Q. (2005). *The on-track indicator as a predictor of high school graduation.* Chicago, IL: Consortium on Chicago School Research, University of Chicago.

Almeida, C., Steinberg, A., Santos, J., & Le, C. (2010). *Six pillars of effective dropout prevention and recovery: An assessment of current state policy and how to improve it.* Retrieved from http://files.eric.ed.gov/fulltext/ED520000.pdf

Atkins, T. (2008). Is alternative school a school of choice? It depends. *Journal of School Choice, 2*(3), 344-347.

Balfanz, R., Almeida, C., Steinberg, A., Santos, J., & Fox, J. H. (2009). *Graduating America: Meeting the challenge of low graduation-rate high schools.* Washington, DC: Jobs for the Future.

Bandura, A. (1977a). Self-efficacy: Toward a unifying theory of behavioral change. *Psychological review, 84*(2), 191.

Bandura, A. (1977b). *Social learning theory.* Englewood Cliffs, NJ: Prentice-Hall.

Blomeyer, R. (2002). *Virtual schools and e-learning in K-12 environments: Emerging policy and practice.* Naperville, IL: North Central Regional Educational Laboratory.

Biddle, J., & Saha, L. (2005). *The untested accusation: Principals, research, knowledge, and policy making.* Westport, CT: Ablex.

Brown v. Board of Education of Topeka, 347 U.S. 483. (1954)

Bruner, J. (1985). Vygotsky: A historical and conceptual perspective. In J. Wertsch, (Ed.), *Culture, communication and cognition: Vygotskyan perspectives* (pp. 162-178). New York, NY: Cambridge University Press.

Buchanan, N. K., & Fox, R. A. (2008). Every school a school of choice: school choice in Ireland as viewed through American eyes. *Irish Educational Studies, 27*(3), 267-279.

Bullock, L. M. (2007). Introduction to the special issue: Ensuring student success through alternative schools. *Preventing School Failure: Alternative Education for Children and Youth, 51*(2), 3-4.

Cavanaugh, C. S. (2001). The effectiveness of interactive distance education technologies in K-12 learning: A meta-analysis. *International Journal of Educational Telecommunications, 7*(1), 73-88.

Chang, L., & Terry, R. (2007). *Wisdom for the soul of Black folk.* Washington DC: Gnosophia Publishers.

Christenson, S., Rounds, T., & Gorney, D. (1992, Fall). *Family factors and student achievement: An avenue to increase students' success* [serial online]. *School Psychology Quarterly, 7*(3), 178-206.

Christie, K. (2008). An exponential payoff. *Phi Delta Kappan, 89*(5), 325-326.

Conley, B. (2002). *Alternative schools: A reference handbook.* Santa Barbara, CA: ABC-CLIO.

Creswell, J. W. (2003). *Research design: Qualitative, quantitative, and mixed methods approaches* (2nd ed.). Thousand Oaks, CA: SAGE.

Creswell, J. W. (2005). *Educational research: Planning, conducting, and evaluating quantitative and qualitative research.* Upper Saddle River, NJ: Merrill.

Creswell, J. W. (2008). *Research design: Qualitative, quantitative, and mixed methods approaches* (3rd ed.). Thousand Oaks, CA: SAGE.

Creswell, J. W. (2012). *Educational research: Planning, conducting, and evaluating quantitative and qualitative research* (4th ed.). Upper Saddle River, NJ: Pearson.

Creswell, J. W. (2013). *Qualitative inquiry and research design: Choose among five approaches* (3rd ed.). Thousand Oaks, CA: Sage.

Creswell, J. W., Hanson, W. E., Plano, V. L. C., & Morales, A. (2007). Qualitative research designs selection and implementation. *The Counseling Psychologist, 35*(2), 236-264.

D'Angelo, F., & Zemanick, R. (2009). The twilight academy: An alternative education program that works. *Preventing School Failure, 51*(4), 211-218.

De La Ossa, P. (2005). Hear my voice: Alternative high school students' perceptions and implications for school change. *American Secondary Education, 34*(1), 24-39.

Dessoff, A. (2009). Reaching graduation with credit-recovery. *District Administration, 45*(9), 43-48.

Dewey, J. (1938). *Experience and education.* New York, NY: Simon & Schuster.

Dornbusch, S. M., & Ritter, P. L. (1988). Parents of high school students: A neglected resource. *Educational Horizons,* 75-77.

Downing, J., & Harrison, T. (1990). Dropout prevention: A practical Approach. *School Counselor, 38*(1), 67-74.

Dray, B. J., & Basler Wisneski, D. (2011). Mindful reflection as a process for developing culturally responsive practices. *Teaching Exceptional Children, 44*(1), 28.

Ellison, T., & Trickett, E. (2006). Environmental structure and the perceived similarity-satisfaction relationship: Traditional and alternative schools. *Journal of Personality, 46*(1), 57-71.

Feinberg, C. (2004). *The possible dream: A nation of proficient school children.* Retrieved from http://www.gse.harvard.edu/news/ed/04/07/possible-dream

Fontana, A., & Frey, J. (2005). The interview: From neutral stance to political involvement. In N. Denzin & Y. Lincoln (Eds.), *Handbook of qualitative inquiry* (3rd ed., pp. 695-728). Thousand Oaks, CA: Sage.

Franco, M. S., & Patel, N. H. (2011). An interim report on a pilot credit-recovery program in a large, suburban midwestern high school. *Education, 132*(1), 15-27.

Franklin, C. (1992). Alternative school programs for at-risk youths. *Social Work in Education, 14*(4), 239-251.

Fullan, M. (2001). *Leading in a culture of change.* San Francisco, CA: John Wiley & Sons.

Gable, R. A., Bullock, L. M., & Evans, W. H. (2006). Changing perspectives on alternative schooling for children and adolescents with challenging behavior. *Preventing School Failure, 51*(1), 5-9.

Gagné, M., & Deci, E. L. (2005). Self-determination theory and work motivation. *Journal of Organizational Behavior, 26*(4), 331-362.

Giorgi, A. (2012). The descriptive phenomenological psychological method. *Journal of Phenomenological Psychology, 43*(1), 3-12.

Gregg, S. (1999). Creating effective alternatives for disruptive students. *Clearinghouse House, 72*(3), 107-114.

Hayes, D., & Singh, A. (2012). *Qualitative inquiry in clinical and educational setting.* New York, NY: The Guilford Press.

Harvey, J., Holland, H., & Hensley, D. (2012). *The school principal as the leader: Guiding schools to better teaching and learning.* New York, NY: The Wallace Foundation.

Heckman, J. J., & LaFontaine, P. A. (2010). The American high school graduation rate: Trends and levels. *The Review of Economics and Statistics, 92*(2), 244-262.

Hoyle, D. (1998). Constructions of pupil absence in the British education service. *Child & Family Social Work, 3*(2), 99-111.

Hughes-Hassell, S. (2008). What can we learn from them? *Knowledge Quest, 37*(1), 9-11.

Iachini, A. L., Buettner, C., Anderson-Butcher, D., & Reno, R. (2013). Exploring students' perceptions of academic disengagement and reengagement in a dropout recovery charter school setting. *Children & Schools, 35*(2), 113.

Keller, E. (2014) The slowdown in American educational attainment. *Journal of Economic Dynamics and Control 46*, 252-270.

Kennelly, L., & Monrad, M. (2007, October). *Approaches to dropout prevention: Heeding early warning signs with appropriate interventions.* Washington, DC: National High School Center at the American Institutes for Research.

Khalifa, M. (2011). Teacher expectations about principal behavior responding to teacher acquiescence. *Urban Review, 43*(5), 702-727.

Kim, J., & Taylor, K. (2008). Rethinking alternative education to break the cycle of educational inequality and inequity. *Journal of Educational Research, 101*(4), 207-219.

Kronholz, J. (2011). Getting at-risk teens to graduation: Blended learning offers a second chance. *Education Next, 11*(4), 24-31.

Kuykendall, C. (2004). *From rage to hope.* New York, NY: Solution Tree.

Ladson-Billings, G. (2009). *The dreamkeepers: Successful teachers of African American children.* San Francisco, CA: Wiley Imprint.

Lange, C. M., & Sletten, S. J. (2002). *Alternative education: A brief history and research synthesis.* Retrieved from http://sde.idaho.gov/site/alternative_schools/docs/alt/alternative_ed_history%202002

Lagana-Riordan, C., Aguilar, J. P., Franklin, C., Streeter, C. L., Kim, J. S., Tripodi, S. J., & Hopson, L. M. (2011). At-risk students' perceptions of traditional schools and a solution-focused public alternative school. *Preventing School Failure, 55*(3), 105-114.

LaRocque, M., Kleiman, I., & Darling, S. (2011). Parent involvement: The missing link in school achievement. *Preventing School Failure, 55*(3), 115-122.

Lehr, C. A., Lanners, E. J., & Lange, C. M. (2003). *Alternative schools: Policy and legislation across the United States. Research Report 1.* Minneapolis, MN: Alternative Schools Research Project, Institute on Community Integration University of Minnesota

Lehr, C. A., Moreau, R. A., Lange, C. M., & Lanners, E. J. (2004). *Alternative schools: Findings from a national survey of the states: Research report 2*. Minneapolis, MN: Institute on Community Integration.

Lehr, C., & Lange, C. (2003) Alternative schools serving students with and without disabilities: What are the current issues and challenges? [serial online]. *Preventing School Failure, 47*(2), 59-65.

Lloyd, S. C. (2007). Ninth-grade is key in graduation pipeline. *Education Week, 27*(8). Retrieved from http://www.edweek.org/rc/articles/2007/10/03/sow1003.h27.html

McIntyre-Bhatty, K. (2008). Truancy and coercive consent: Is there an alternative? *Educational Review, 60*(1), 375-390.

McKee, J., & Conner, E. (2007) Alternative schools, mainstream education. *Principal Leadership, 8*(4), 44-49.

McLeod, S. (2007). Maslow's hierarchy of needs. *Simply Psychology*. Retrieved from http://www.ouchihs.org/apps/download/2/NghLRUHA09y-cRFi190Zws5youGeihn81UYVGpHLCukqjXEs1.pdf/Maslow's%20Hierarchy%20of%20Needs.pdf

McNulty, C., & Roseboro, D. (2009). I'm not really that bad: Alternative school students, stigma, and identity politics. *Equity and Excellence In Education, 42*(4), 412-427.

McWhirther, J., McWhirther, B., McWhirther, A., & McWhirther, E. (1998). *At risk youth: A comprehensive response*. Pacific Grove, CA: Brooke/Cole Publishing.

Menendez, A. L. (2007). Supports and enhancements designed for alternative school programming. *Preventing School Failure, 51*(2), 19-22.

Merrifield, J., Warne, L., Bentsen, L. IV, O'Sullivan, C., & Barnett, J. (2013). Private school choice: Options for Texas children. *National Center for Policy Analysis*. Retrieved from www.ncpa.org/pub/st345

Miller, C. A., Fitch, T., & Marshall, J. L. (2003). Locus of control and at-risk youth: A comparison of regular education high school students and students in alternative schools. *Education, 123*(3), 548-551.

Monchinski, T. (2008). *Critical pedagogy in the everyday classroom*. New York, NY: Springer.

Mottaz, C. (2002). *Breaking the cycle of failure: How to build and maintain quality alternative schools*. Lanham, MD: Rowman & Littlefield (formerly Scarecrow Press).

Moustakas, C. (1994). *Phenomenological research methods*. Thousand Oaks, CA: Sage Publications.

Nicic, M., Petrovic, E., Sehovic, S., & Hajrovic, E. (2013). Project modernization and reform of education system through the new methods of learning. *TTEM-Technics Technologies Education Management, 8*(1), 260-263.

Pemberton, B. (2011, April). *Supporting credit recovery students to find success.* TCC 2011 Worldwide Online Conference. Retrieved from http://scholarspace.manoa.hawaii.edu/bitstream/handle/10125/19946/beth_pemberton_tccconference_presentation.pdf?sequence=2

Pipho, C. (2000). Choice options on the increase. *Phi Delta Kappan, 81*(8), 565-566.

Quinn, M. M., Poirier, J. M., Faller, S. E., Gable, R. A., & Tonelson, S. W. (2006). An examination of school climate in effective alternative programs. *Preventing School Failure, 51*(1), 11-17.

Ravitch, S. M., & Wirth, K. (2007). Developing a pedagogy of opportunity for students and their teachers Navigations and negotiations in insider action research. *Action Research, 5*(1), 75-91.

Raywid, M. A. (1989). *The case for public schools of choice.* Fastback 283. Bloomington, IN: Phi Delta Kappa Educational Foundation.

Riehl, C. (2000). The principal's role in creating inclusive schools for diverse students: A review of normative, empirical, and critical literature on the practice of educational administration. *Educational Research, (70)*, 55-81.

Ripley, A. (2013). *The smartest kids in the world: And how they got that way.* New York, NY: Simon and Schuster.

Ritchie, J., & Lewis, J. (2003). *A guide for social science students and researchers.* Thousand Oaks, CA: Sage.

Rix, J., & Twining, P. (2007). Talking about schools: Towards a typology for future education. *Educational Research, 48*(4), 329-341.

Roblyer, M. D. (2008). Virtual schools: Redefining "a place called school." In J. Voogt & G. Knezek (Eds.), *International handbook of information technology in primary and secondary education* (pp. 695-711). New York, NY: Springer US.

Roosevelt, R. (1999). *Building a house for diversity.* New York, NY: American Management Association.

Rumberger, R. W. (2001). *Why students drop out of school and what can be done.* Retrieved from http://civilrightsproject.ucla.edu/research/k-12-education/school-dropouts/why-students-drop-out-of-school-and-what-can-be-done/rumberger-why-students-dropout-2001.pdf

Rumberger, R. W. (2011). *Dropping out.* Cambridge, MA: Harvard University Press.

Ryan, R. M., & Deci, E. L. (2000). Self-determination theory and the facilitation of intrinsic motivation, social development, and well-being. *American Psychologist, 55*(1), 68.

Sagor, R. (1999). Equity and excellence in public schools: The role of the alternative school. *The Clearing House, 73*(2), 72-75.

Scott, J. (2012). Educational movements, not market moments. *Dissent, 59*(1), 72-75.

Sheldon, S. B. (2002). Parents' social networks and beliefs as predictors of parent involvement. *The Elementary School Journal, 102*(4), 301-316.

Simons, J. A., Irwin, D. B., & Drinnien, B. A. (1987). *Maslow's hierarchy of needs.* Retrieved from http://scholar.google.co.uk/scholar?hl=en&q= Simons%2C J. A.%2C Irwin%2CD. B.%2C %26 Drinnien%2C B. A. %281987%29. Maslow%E2%80%99s hierarchyof needs&btnG=&as_sdt=1%2C5&as_sdtp

Siwatu, S. (2011). Preservice teachers' culturally responsive teaching self-efficacy-forming experiences: A mixed methods study. *The Journal of Educational Research, 104*(5), 360-369.

Stake, R. (2005). Qualitative case studies. In N. Denzin & Y. Lincoln (Eds.), *Handbook of qualitative research* (3rd ed., pp. 443-466). Thou- sand Oaks, CA: Sage.

Steinberg, A., & Almeida, C. A. (2008). *Raising graduation rates in an era of high standards: Five commitments for state action.* Retrieved from http://files.eric.ed.gov/ fulltext/ED500541.pdf

Streeter, C. L., Franklin, C., Kim, J. S., & Tripodi, S. J. (2011). Concept mapping: An approach for evaluating a public alternative school program. *Children & Schools, 33*(4), 197-214.

Stromquist, N. P. (2002). *Education in a globalized world: The connectivity of economic power, technology, and knowledge.* Boulder, CO: Rowman & Littlefield Publishers.

Tesch, R. (1990). *Qualitative research: Analysis types and software tools.* Psychology Press.

Texas Education Agency. (2009). *Building the longitudinal cohort used for calculating completion rates.* Retrieved from http://tea.texas.gov/acctres/DropComp_Present_TAC_Dec_9_2008.pdf

Texas Education Agency. (2013). *Grade-level retention and student performance in Texas public schools, 2010-11* (Document No. GE13 601 04). Austin TX: Author.

Trautman, T., & Lawrence, J. (2004). Credit recovery: A technology-based intervention for dropout prevention at Wichita Falls High School. *Oklahoma City: American Education Corporation.* Retrieved from http://www.coloradocourseward .com/pdf/Research_Digest_Cred.pdf

Trickett, E. J., McConahay, J. B., Phillips, D., & Ginter, M. A. (1985). Natural experiments and the educational context: The environment and effects of an alternative inner-city public school on adolescents. *American Journal of Community Psychology, 13*(6), 617-643.

Trotter, A. (2008). Online options for 'credit recovery' widen. *Education Week, 27*(38), 1.

Tyler, J., & Lofstrom, M. (2009). Finishing high school: Alternative pathways and dropout recovery. *Future of Children, 19*(1), 77-103.

Vadeboncoeur, J. (2009). Spaces of difference: The contradictions of alternative educational programs. *Educational Studies, 45,* 280-299.

Washburn, J. (2004). Credit-recovery program helps at-risk students meet promotional requirements. *Technological Horizons in Education, 32*(1), 42-43.

Watson, J. (2005). *Keeping pace with K-12 online learning: A review of state-level policy and practice.* Retrieved from http://files.eric.ed.gov/fulltext/ED489514.pdf

Watson, J., & Gemin, B. (2008). Promising practices in online learning: Using online learning for at-risk students and credit recovery. *North American Council for Online Learning.* Retrieved from www.k12hsn.org/files/.../NACOL_Credit-Recovery_PromisingPractices.p...for At-Risk Students and. Credit Recovery.

Weck, C. (2008). Brainology: Transforming students' motivation to learn. *Independent Schools, 67*(2), 1-7.

Woldt, A., & Toman, S. (2005). *Gestalt therapy: History, theory, and practice.* Thousand Oaks, CA: Sage Publications, Inc.

Wolk, R. (2010). The case for making it personal. *Educational Leadership, 67*(7), 16-21.

Wright, L. (2012) Restructuring public education for the 21st century. *National Center for Policy Analysis.* Retrieved from http://www.ncpa.org/pub/ib107

Yuanying, W. (2011). College English writing on scaffolding theory. *Studies in Literature and Language, 3*(3), 46-48.

Zepeda, S. J. (2004). *Instructional leadership for school improvement.* Larchmont, NY: Eye on Education.

Zehr, M. (2010). Demand still growing for online credit recovery classes. *Education Week, 29*(36), 10. Retrieved from http://www.edweek.org/ew/articles/2010/07/14/36credit-2.h29.html?tkn=LSRFI4cEw36I26b3LVSZHylt4Yxl-vSnVeHZt&print=1

Zimmerman, B. J., Bandura, A., & Martinez-Pons, M. (1992). Self-motivation for academic attainment: The role of self-efficacy beliefs and personal goal setting. *American Educational Research Journal, 29*(3), 663-676.

Zinth, J. D. (2011). Credit recovery and proficiency-based credit: Maintaining high expectations while providing flexibility. *Education Commission of the States.* Retrieved from http://www.ecs.org/clearinghouse/94/23/9423.pdf#sthash.24tuoWfs.dpuf